THE ABINGDON WORSHIP ANNUAL

2006

CONTEMPORARY & TRADITIONAL
RESOURCES FOR WORSHIP LEADERS

The

ABINGDON
WORSHIP
Annual
2006

EDITED BY MARY J. SCIFRES & B. J. BEU
FOREWORD BY DAVID BUECHLER AND MARY J. SCIFRES

Abingdon Press
Nashville

THE ABINGDON WORSHIP ANNUAL 2006
CONTEMPORARY AND TRADITIONAL RESOURCES FOR WORSHIP LEADERS

Copyright © 2005 by Abingdon Press

This book is printed on acid-free paper.

ISBN 0-687-06249-7

05 06 07 08 09 10 11 12 13 14—10 9 8 7 6 5 4 3 2 1

MANUFACTURED IN THE UNITED STATES OF AMERICA

CONTENTS

1950

111224

OCTOBER

NOVEMBER

DECEMBER

FOREWORD

How do we understand worship? Worship is the act of giving our praise, adoration, and full attention *to God*. When we worship, we acknowledge the power of God, the grace of Christ, and the guidance of the Holy Spirit. We may pray, sing, dance, clap, proclaim, and hear God's word, or silently meditate.

And yet, this traditional understanding of worship is becoming lost today in many of our churches, where worship has become a sort of spectator sport. In some churches, people come to our church buildings to have personal needs met or to sing favorite songs. They come to be fed, to receive, to be led into the presence of God by "professionals." They come as if to a performance, choose a favorite seat, evaluate the musicianship, contemplate the quality of the preacher, hobnob with other attendees, and then file out with their programs, as if they had just gone to the theater or the symphony.

The whole idea of coming to a service of worship for the purpose of receiving is a relatively new phenomenon. It is only recently that the worship service has been so nonparticipatory. Historically, Christians have known that worship is designed to be a "full-body" experience. *The Abingdon Worship Annual* is a resource designed to help worship planners design services that encourage people to enter into this "full-body" experience.

As we reflect on what it means to be full participants in worship, two scriptural images come to mind. The first is the image of relating to the Holy One along a vertical axis. After all, we are called to love the Lord our God with all our heart, soul, strength, and mind (Deuteronomy 6:5; Matthew

9

22:37; Luke 10:27). All that we have and have not, all that we are and are not, all that we have become and are becoming, everything that comprises our heart, soul, strength, and mind, all these belong to God. We bring our whole selves to worship, not just a piece of ourselves. Our joys and our sorrows, our happiness and our anger, our laughter and our tears, our songs and our shouts exist to give God glory. Psalm 95 is an eloquent depiction of our human need to worship God with praise and thanksgiving, with songs and prayers and with our very lives. This is our physical body's commitment to the Holy One and our true spiritual worship.

The second scriptural image of what it means to be full participants in worship is the image of relating to one another within the Body of Christ along a horizontal axis. The Body of Christ is called together for the worship of God. Wherever two or three are gathered, Christ promises to be in our midst (Matthew 18:20). Paul reminds us that each member of the body plays an important role in the worship and ministry of Christ on this earth (Romans 12:4-8). Worship is an invitation for each member to bring his or her contribution to the act of worship. Clearly, God did not design worship to be a spectator sport. God yearns for our total engagement in the act of worship, not only with God, but with each other as well. Worship is an invitation to engage with Christ's Body and with Christ in a personal and intimate way. Worship is an opportunity to give God glory as we declare together the worth and honor that belongs to Christ.

As we prepare to partake of this amazing gift, we are invited into another amazing gift—the gift of planning worship. As your worship plans emerge, imagine a worship experience filled with participants just as actively engaged in worship as the planners and leaders. Imagine a time of worship in which humans are as intimately engaged in worship as God's very self is engaged with us, in worship and at all times. Imagine a time when the worshipers remember: Our reason for being is to worship. God made us to worship, Christ redeemed us to worship, the Holy Spirit guides us to worship. It is the whole of God. It should be the whole of us.

David Buechler and Mary J. Scifres

INTRODUCTION

Worship planning is a dangerous venture. It brings with it many of the typical challenges of local church ministry—volunteer availability, personal preferences, staffing needs, and time limitations. But it also brings with it an additional host of challenges, due to the sacred and intimate nature of worship. Worshipers can be brought to tears by amazing words and music; they can also be driven to fits of rage over the same words and music. Personal preferences reach a new level of importance in the minds of people for whom communal worship is the single most sacred moment of the week. For better or for worse, you are invited into this sacred art, whether as pastor, as musician, as worship leader, or as a planning volunteer.

There is much about worship planning that is deeply rewarding. Within the act of planning, we pray and study. We search and discern for words and worship acts that will bring people to the heights of joy or to the introspective depths of true repentance. We plan services that evoke laughter or awe. We discover new prayers, or old twists on familiar scriptures, or unusual arrangements of favorite hymns that excite and energize us. And then, as the congregation gathers to worship, we offer our best plans and hopes and dreams to God.

One of the great challenges in planning worship is how people respond to the Holy. No matter how carefully worship is planned, the congregation's response can never be controlled. And yet, that response is the very thing that makes worship precious to our Creator—it is in our individual and communal response to God that lives are transformed and healed. In our response as worshipers, the planning disappears from view as the worship of God moves into central place. Good worship planning facilitates this focus upon God; bad worship planning distracts focus away from God. In even the best-planned services, however, a congregation's focus might be irretrievably elsewhere. When this happens, worship planners may become discouraged. And yet, the Holy Spirit is moving still. We can no more control the Spirit than we can control the congregation: "The Spirit blows where it will" (John 3:8, paraphrased). And the congregation worships as it will.

We also know that pastors and worship leaders are often overwhelmed with the time-consuming and awesome task of planning weekly worship. In particular, the need to plan multiple services of varying or blended styles can weigh down the most lighthearted and joy-filled planner. To help you and your worship team plan thematically coherent, lectionary based worship services each week, we offer you this invaluable planning resource. For when worship arises from careful and caring plans, God is honored and glorified, and Christ is praised and worshiped. When worship is approached faithfully and prayerfully, with careful planning and with an eye given to detail, the congregation is better able to experience the Spirit's presence in their midst.

And so, we offer you *The Abingdon Worship Annual*. With this resource, we hope to fill a void in your worship-planning library. *The Abingdon Worship Annual* offers liturgical resources for both traditional and contemporary worship. In it, you will find suggestions in both traditional and contemporary style for each Sunday of the year (and most holy days), to help plan your corporate worship services. Each entry includes: Calls to Worship, Opening Prayers, Praise Sentences, Contemporary Gathering Words, Prayers of Confession or Unison Prayers, and Benedictions. The Praise Sentences and Contemporary Gathering Words fit the spontaneous and informal nature of many nontraditional worship styles. These are particularly helpful to those leading contemporary worship. The Calls to Worship, Unison Prayers, and Benediction are more traditional in style, and yet, many of these entries are adaptable for any style of worship. In all cases, the readings are scripture-referenced and lectionary-based.

You may notice that *The Abingdon Worship Annual* was written to complement *The Abingdon Preaching Annual*. But *The Abingdon Worship Annual* is also well used alongside *Prepare! A Weekly Worship Planbook for Pastors and Musicians*, or *The United Methodist Music and Worship Planner*. Together, this trinity of resources provides the music, the words, and the preaching guidance to plan integrated and coordinated worship services.

All contributions in *The Abingdon Worship Annual* are based upon readings from the Revised Common Lectionary. As you begin your worship planning, we encourage you to spend time with the scriptures for the day, reflecting upon them thoughtfully and prayerfully. Then, read through the many offerings in this resource that speak to those scriptures. Listen for the words that speak to you. Since the contributing authors represent a wide variety of denominational and theological backgrounds, the words before you will vary in style and content. Let this resource be the starting point for your worship planning, letting the Spirit guide you and allowing God's word to flow through you. Feel free to combine or adjust the words within these pages to fit the needs of your congregation and the style of your worship services. Trust God's guidance, and enjoy a wonderful year of worship and praise with your congregations!

As you work with the 2006 edition of the *Abingdon Worship Annual*, some explanations may be helpful in using it to the fullest. Calls to Worship are words that gather God's people together as they prepare to worship. These words of greeting or gathering are typically read responsively. Some of the Contemporary Gathering Words listed in each resource may also be helpful as Calls to Worship in traditional or blended-worship settings. As with all responsive readings, think creatively as you plan your services. While it is simplest to have a single leader read the words in light print, having the congregation respond by reading the words in bold print, it is often effective to have several people, or even groups of people, lead these calls. Using the choir, or a youth group, or a small prayer group, adds variety and vitality to your services. Some congregations enjoy responding to one another: women to men, right side to left side, children to parents. Experiment with a variety of options, and see how these words might be most meaningful in calling your congregation together to worship the Holy One.

Like more formal Calls to Worship, Contemporary Gathering Words are often read responsively. Unlike more formal Calls to Worship, however, Contemporary Gathering Words tend to use simpler language and are typically more repetitive in nature. You may copy any and all entries onto an overhead transparency to help your congregation read responsively without being tied to a bulletin. If your congregation does not care to read words aloud, consider using two leaders to speak in "call and response" format. Or, allow the song team or band members to act as responders to the worship leader, echoing the call and response tradition of African American Christians.

While many of the Praise Sentences provided in this resource are easily spoken by one leader, using the call and response format is an option. In praise settings, worshipers are often willing to respond in echo form, repeating the words or phrases spoken by the worship leader. Echoing the same words and phrases several times can be highly effective. The Praise Sentences in this resource are not intended to limit you, but rather to free you to lead in a more informal and free-flowing style, where appropriate.

Opening Prayers in this resource are varied in form, but typically invoke God's presence in worship. Some are more informal than others, and some are more general than formal invocations. Opening prayers may be read by a single worship leader or by the whole congregation in unison. Many can be adapted for later use in the worship service, if that suits your needs. For the sake of simplicity, we have grouped them all into the category of Opening Prayers.

Other prayers take many forms in this resource. Some are offered as Prayers of Confession. Confessional prayers and their corresponding Words of Assurance follow many different formats. At times, the Assurance of Pardon is contained in the prayer. When it is not, you may wish to use Words of Assurance from a previous day's suggested resources or from a favorite scripture of assurance. Some prayers are in the form of a Collect. Some of these prayers may even be adapted as Opening or Closing Prayers. Any prayer may be revised into call and response format. In all cases, we have sought to provide words that can easily be spoken by a large congregation in unison. For the sake of consistency, such entries have been given the title, Unison Prayer. You may use any title you deem appropriate in your worship bulletins.

Benedictions, sometimes known as Blessings or Words of Dismissal, are included in each entry. Some work best in call and response format; others seem more appropriate as a solitary blessing from the worship leader. Choose a format best suited to your congregation.

Many litanies, prayers, and calls to worship in *The Abingdon Worship Annual 2006* intersperse direct quotations from scripture with lines of text for other sources. In order to facilitate the ease of use with this resource, we have chosen not to indicate in the prayers and other worship resources where scripture is being directly quoted and where it is not.

Enjoy this resource, and enjoy the year ahead. We wish you God's blessings as you seek to share Christ's word and offer experiences of the Holy Spirit in your work and worship!

Mary J. Scifres and B. J. Beu, Editors

JANUARY 1, 2006

First Sunday after Christmas
Mary J. Scifres

COLOR
White

SCRIPTURE READINGS
Isaiah 61:10–62:3; Psalm 148; Galatians 4:4-7; Luke 2:22-40

THEME IDEAS
On the cusp of celebrating Epiphany, light and revelation come to the forefront on this last Sunday of Christmas. Isaiah's proclamation of God's adornments is surely seen in the beautiful garments of Christmas celebrations throughout the world. The psalmist's invitation for the whole earth to sing God's praises reflects our joyous outbursts at the good news of Christmas. But, most of all, Galatians and Luke point to the fullness of salvation that was revealed and realized in Jesus' birth on this earth. Indeed, every fiber of our existence should exult in God (Isaiah 61:1)!

CALL TO WORSHIP (PSALM 148)
Hear the angels ...
praising our God in the highest heavens!
See the sun and the moon ...
shining with the glory of God!

Gaze upon the glittering stars . . .
where God's wisdom gleams with pleasure.
Listen to the wind and the waves . . .
for they sing of the power of God!
Hear the creatures of the deep . . .
praising our God from the darkest waters!
See the animals of the earth . . .
singing praise with their mysterious sounds.
Gaze upon the majestic mountains . . .
where God's strength stands with dignity.
Listen to the storms of fire and rain . . .
cry with the awesomeness of God.
Young and old, women and men, sing with the earth.
Praise and glory, honor and joy belong to God!
Hallelujah for Christ has come!

CALL TO WORSHIP (ISAIAH 61)

Rejoice in Christ Jesus, the beauty of God.
We sing of the One who clothes us with joy.
Rejoice in Christ Jesus, the light of salvation.
We worship the One who wraps us in grace.
Rejoice in Christ Jesus, the hope of new life.
We worship the One who blesses us with hope.
Rejoice in Christ Jesus, the One who is here.
We worship the Christ, God's love in our midst.

CONTEMPORARY GATHERING WORDS (CHRISTMAS, NEW YEAR, ISAIAH 61)

This is a season of hope, a season of grace.
This is a day of new beginnings
    when we celebrate the promise, begun with a child,
    embraced by a man, and fulfilled in the Christ.
As we enter this new year, may this season
    of hope and grace remain in our hearts
    and call us to rejoice in the promise of the days ahead.

CONTEMPORARY GATHERING WORDS (PSALM 148)

Praise God with angels and kings.
Praise God with the sun and the moon.
Praise God with the stars and the heavens.
Praise God with the birds and the beasts.
Praise God with the storms and the desert.
Praise God with the trees and the fields.
Praise God with mountains and oceans.
Let everything and everyone sing praise to God!

PRAISE SENTENCES (CHRISTMAS, PSALM 148)

Christ is born! Hallelujah!
Christ is born! Hallelujah!
Glory to God in the highest heavens!
Glory to God on this earth!

OPENING PRAYER (GALATIANS 4, LUKE 2)

Holy and loving God,
    in the fullness of time,
    you revealed yourself to us
        as the Christ Child.
Reveal yourself to us again
    that we may know and trust your promises
    with the faith and strength
        of Anna and Simeon.
And as Jesus grew in strength and wisdom,
    so may we grow in the strength and wisdom
    of your holy Word. Amen.

OPENING PRAYER (NEW YEAR, GALATIANS 4)

On this first day of the New Year,
    breathe upon us with the breath of your Spirit.
Fill our hearts with your love
    and ignite our souls
        with the fire of your passion.

Embrace us as your children
that we may embrace this new year
as your faithful disciples,
servants of love and grace.
In your gentle and loving name,
we pray, dear Abba! Father!
Amen and amen!

CLOSING PRAYER (LUKE 2)

Ruler of our hearts,
let us now leave this place
in the peace of your love.
As we have seen and heard your salvation
in this holy season,
let us share that life-giving good news
with a world yearning for light and life.
As your people, we pray. Amen.

BENEDICTION (LUKE 2)

Let us now depart in peace.
Let us leave with the light of truth.
Let us depart with trust and hope.
Let us leave with the faith of children.
Let us depart with Christmas joy!
Let us leave with Christmas love!

JANUARY 6, 2006

Epiphany of the Lord
B. J. Beu

COLOR
White

SCRIPTURE READINGS
Isaiah 60:1-6; Psalm 72:1-7, 10-14; Ephesians 3:1-12; Matthew 2:1-12

THEME IDEAS
Evidence of Jesus' messiahship abounds in today's readings. When the Messiah comes, the Gentiles will stop worshiping idols, and start worshiping the one true God, the God of Israel. Isaiah proclaims that the light of God has come to the nations, and at last, the nations have come to God's light. Gold and frankincense have indeed been brought by Gentile kings to a new king—the one who is the very light of the world. Paul considers himself a prisoner of the gospel so that the Gentiles might be brought to the boundless riches of Christ.

CALL TO WORSHIP (ISAIAH 60)
Arise, shine, for your light has come.
The glory of the Lord has risen upon us!
Behold, the nations have come to witness God's light.
Kings have come to behold Christ's brightness.
Lift up your eyes and look around.
The glory of the Lord has come!

CALL TO WORSHIP (PSALM 72)

O God, your justice rolls down like waters,
your righteousness like an ever-flowing stream.
You deliver the needy when they call.
You hear the voice of the poor and the helpless.
You have delivered us, O God,
and we proclaim your glory to the nations.

CALL TO WORSHIP (PSALM 72)

Our God is king.
Let all who oppress the poor tremble.
Our God is righteous.
Let the sinner repent and return to the Lord.
Our God is just.
Let all those who love God shout for joy.
Our God is king.
Let us worship the king of glory.

CONTEMPORARY GATHERING WORDS (ISAIAH 60, MATTHEW 2)

Look around you. God's light shines in the darkness.
The darkness has lifted from our eyes.
Look around you. God's glory is all around us.
Our hearts are filled with joy.
Look around you. Christ's star is risen in the sky.
We will follow this star
to discover the light of the world.

PRAISE SENTENCES (MATTHEW 2)

Our king has come!
Bring Christ gifts of gold, frankincense, and myrrh.
Our king has come!
Bring Christ gifts of love and joy.
Our king has come!
Bring Christ gifts of praise and worship.

OPENING PRAYER (MATTHEW 2)

Glorious God,
you are nearer to us than our very breath,
yet we often fail to see you in
our everyday lives.
Grant us the courage to follow your light,
wherever you would lead us.
May we follow the kings of old,
as they followed the star
to find the infant Jesus.
Help us give of ourselves,
that we may forsake the glitter
of things that do not endure,
for the brightness of life eternal,
found in our Savior, Jesus Christ.
Amen.

OPENING PRAYER OR PRAYER OF CONFESSION (MATTHEW 2)

Eternal God,
kings of old left their homelands and their own people,
to follow a star and find a foreigner
whose birth was so profound,
it was proclaimed in the heavens above.
Forgive our feet of clay,
when we would rather sit comfortably in our homes,
than venture forth to follow your guidance in our lives.
Help us follow the example of the Magi,
who brought precious gifts
of gold, frankincense , and myrrh,
to honor the King of kings.
Teach us to open our shut-up hearts
to those in need around us,
through the one who brought light into our lives. Amen.

ASSURANCE OF PARDON (EPHESIANS 3)

The power that brought light and salvation to the
Gentiles
> is at work in the world today,
> granting eternal life to those who turn to God.

The power of the living God
> transforms our hearts of stone
> into hearts that sing with gladness.

BENEDICTION (ISAIAH 60, PSALM 72)

Go forth as a light to the nations.
We go forth, following the star of Christ's birth.
Go forth as a people of blessing.
We go forth, proclaiming hope
to the poor and needy.
Go forth as a light to the nations.
We go forth, with God's blessings.

BENEDICTION (MATTHEW 2)

Follow the kings of old in search of God's Son.
We go with the promise of new life in Christ.
Follow the Magi in search of the promise of heaven.
We go with the promise of new life in Christ.

JANUARY 8, 2006

Baptism of the Lord

Bryan Schneider-Thomas

COLOR
White

SCRIPTURE READINGS
Genesis 1:1-5; Psalm 29; Acts 19:1-7; Mark 1:4-11

THEME IDEAS
In the waters of baptism, we die to ourselves and are recreated through the Holy Spirit into the Body of Christ. Water can be threatening (a flood or a powerful current), refreshing (a cool drink on a hot summer day), or invigorating (a morning shower or a swim in cool water). The various experiences of water in our own life allude to the diversity of perspectives in the texts today and in baptism itself. It would be appropriate to invite people to experience and encounter water in some way as a reminder of their baptism or as an invitation for baptism.

CALL TO WORSHIP (PSALM 29)
The voice of the Lord—Strong and Mighty,
powerful and full of majesty.
It calls to us, calling across the water.
The voice of the Lord breaks forth.
It gives us strength and blessing, causing us to shout "Glory to the name of the Lord!"

CALL TO WORSHIP (MARK 1)
Lost ...
wandering without purpose, meaning, value, acceptance, or place.
We wander lost. But the Spirit of God descends like a dove upon us. We hear the ancient words that name and claim us as children of God.
We are cleansed, refreshed, and made new in the love of those words.

CONTEMPORARY GATHERING WORDS
Water. Refreshing, cleansing, nourishing, life-giving ...
Water. Dangerous, life-threatening, powerful ...
The waters rush over us in our baptism.
And we are filled with the Holy Spirit. Alleluia!

PRAISE SENTENCES
Proclaim the glory and strength of God!
The Spirit of creation has recreated us.
Rejoice in the Holy Spirit who gives us life.
We remember our baptism and are thankful.
God has blessed us.

OPENING PRAYER (MARK 1)
Almighty God,
parent of all who call upon your name,
in the waters of baptism you have transformed us,
marking us as your children,
and recreating us through the work of your Son
and the power of the Holy Spirit.
**Shower us once more with your grace
that we might be renewed in your spirit,
through Jesus Christ, our Savior. Amen**

OPENING PRAYER (GENESIS 1)

God of creation, who brought forth light from darkness,
> we are your creation.
May your Spirit be with us today
> to sing your praises and tell of your wonders. Amen.

OPENING PRAYER (MARK 1)

O spirit dove,
> who flew over the chaotic water of creation,
> and alighted upon Jesus in his baptism,
> grace us with your presence.
May we feel the brush of your wings,
> and know that your gift of life is upon us.
Amen.

UNISON PRAYER

Holy God, source of all that is good,
we gather before you seeking your grace and love.
> **Be present in our lives.**
> **Fill us with your light.**
> **Be generous with your love.**
> **Count us among your children.**
> **Be compassionate toward our mistakes.**
> **Forgive our failings.**
> **Be gracious with your power.**
> **Strengthen us for your service.**
We ask these things through the name of Jesus Christ
our Savior, who lives and reigns with you
and the Holy Spirit, one God, now and forever.
> **Amen.**

BENEDICTION

God has laid claim to your life.
By your baptism you have been marked
> as God's own forever.

In grace may God watch over you.
In strength may you go forth in service.

BENEDICTION (PSALM 29)
God is lord over the waters and rules forever.
**May the God who reigns over all creation
give us strength and bless us with peace.**

JANUARY 15, 2006

Second Sunday after the Epiphany
Laura Jaquith Bartlett

COLOR

Green

SCRIPTURE READINGS

1 Samuel 3:1-10 (11-20); Psalm 139:1-6, 13-18; 1 Corinthians 6:12-20; John 1:43-51

THEME IDEAS

Each of these scriptures seems to hold a unique challenge for the preacher and worship planner. The familiar story of God's voice calling to Samuel is muddied by the disturbing tone of God's plan for Eli. The Corinthians passage holds the thorny challenge of preaching on fornication and prostitution, and the Gospel's clear-cut statement about Philip's decision to follow Jesus is juxtaposed against the account of Jesus' somewhat puzzling conversation with Nathanael. But in the midst of this brow-furrowing, the words of Psalm 139 offer comfort to preacher and worshiper alike. God's mystery is indeed too wondrous and complex for us to understand, yet we take refuge in the knowledge that God understands *us*, and loves us still! The mysterious God who calls to us does not abandon us, even when we falter while trying to follow.

CALL TO WORSHIP (1 SAMUEL 3, JOHN 1)
God, you call each of us to serve you, and we answer,
"Here I am!"
Jesus, you call each of us to follow you, and we answer,
"Here I am!"
Holy Spirit, you call each of us to worship you this day,
and we answer,
"Here I am!"

CONTEMPORARY GATHERING WORDS (JOHN 1)
Shhh! Listen! Do you hear it?
**Our ears are filled with the noise of traffic and TV
and video games.**
The call of Jesus is louder than that.
It shouts out above the noise of the world.
Perhaps the signal is too powerful for us to hear.
The call of Jesus is quieter than that.
It whispers in your heart.
We hear it! Praise God!

CONTEMPORARY GATHERING WORDS (JOHN 1, EPIPHANY SEASON)
Come into worship,
and see what God has in store for us today!
We have busy lives, but still, we're curious ...
Come into God's presence,
and see the difference love makes!
**We've been burned by love before,
but still, we're needy ...**
Come into the light and see the glory of God!
**Our eyes have been closed for so long,
but still, we yearn for the light ...**
Come and see! Come and see!

PRAISE SENTENCES (PSALM 139)
We praise you, O God.
You have known us since before we were born.

We love you, O God.
You know us better than we know ourselves.
We worship you, O God.
Your knowledge is more wonderful than we can imagine.
We glorify you, O God.
Your creation is ever-changing and ever-amazing.
We praise you, O God.
Your love is with us forever.

OPENING PRAYER (PSALM 139)

Loving God,
　　you know us better than we know ourselves.
Our prayers are in your heart
　　even before they are on our lips.
And yet we must utter our prayers.
We must proclaim our praise of you
　　and all your wondrous creation.
Your love surrounds us
　　and you have promised to be with us always.
You know our hearts' desire to serve you.
We pray that you will keep us true to that desire.
And so we utter our prayer, in Jesus' name. Amen.

OPENING PRAYER (1 SAMUEL 3)

O God,
　　you call to us today,
　　just as you called to the boy Samuel
　　　　so long ago.
Gathered here today,
　　we are many different ages,
　　but we pray for the maturity of faith
　　　　to hear your call and respond to your Word.
Open our ears and our hearts
　　as we worship, as we work,
　　and as we care for one another.

We ask that you would give us courage and integrity
to answer your call with the heart-felt words,
"Here I am!" Amen.

PRAYER FOR ILLUMINATION (1 SAMUEL 3, JOHN 1)

Open our ears, O God,
that we might hear your Word
speaking to us in this moment.
Open our ears, O God,
that we might listen for your voice
calling to us through scripture.
Open our ears, O God,
that we might understand your promises
to followers both old and young, ancient and modern.
Open our hearts, O God,
that we might enter into the love
you offer us. Amen.

PRAYER OF CONFESSION (PSALM 139)

Awesome God,
you have made all of creation
and each cell of our bodies.
You know our thoughts
and you know our sins.
We desperately try to hide our mistakes,
our weaknesses, our embarrassments.
But you know it all,
and so we come before you now
asking for your forgiveness.
Even as *you* know the limits of our human capabilities,
we know the unlimited power of your love.
Forgive us, cleanse us, make us whole.
(prayer continues in silence)

WORDS OF ASSURANCE (PSALM 139, 1 CORINTHIANS 6)

The God who has made us will never desert us.
The God of creation is creating still, making us new.

The God whose love gave us the gift of Jesus Christ
is the same God whose love forgives and sustains us.
Amen.

BENEDICTION (JOHN 1)

Go into the world, listening for God's call in your lives.
Go into the world, ready to follow Jesus Christ.
Go into the world, sustained by the love and power
of the Holy Spirit. Amen.

BENEDICTION (1 SAMUEL 3, PSALM 139)

And now, sisters and brothers,
go from this place knowing that the God who made you
also sustains you.
The God who calls you also goes with you.
The God who loved you before you were born
still loves you today, and into all the tomorrows. Amen.

JANUARY 22, 2006

Third Sunday after the Epiphany
B. J. Beu

COLOR
Green

SCRIPTURE READINGS
Jonah 3:1-5, 10; Psalm 62:5-12; 1 Corinthians 7:29-31; Mark 1:14-20

THEME IDEAS
Themes of judgment, mercy, promise, and hope abide in today's scripture readings. In Jonah, the Ninevites received warning that they would soon be destroyed, yet when they repented, God held back the wrath in store from them. The psalmist speaks of the soul waiting silently for God and the hope found only in God. Paul speaks of the world's passing and the need to be ready. Finally, Mark's Gospel shows that hope is present when Jesus begins his ministry; even at a time of despair, as John the Baptist is arrested by the authorities.

CALL TO WORSHIP (PSALM 62)
Wait for the Lord. Our souls wait in silent longing.
God alone is our rock and our salvation!
Wait for the Lord. God is our fortress against the storm.
God alone is our rock and our salvation!
Wait for the Lord. God is our refuge and our strength.
God alone is our rock and our salvation!

CALL TO WORSHIP (MARK 1)
Jesus is here, calling us to become his disciples.
We will follow the Lord of life.
Jesus is here, calling us to leave our nets.
We will follow the Lord of life.
Jesus is here, calling us to be fishers of God's children.
We will follow the Lord of life.

CONTEMPORARY GATHERING WORDS (PSALM 62)
How is it with your soul?
For God alone our souls wait in silence.
How is it with your life?
**God has lifted us up, becoming our refuge
and our strength.**

CONTEMPORARY GATHERING WORDS (PSALM 62)
God is our refuge and our strength.
Let the church say amen!
God is the rock of our salvation.
Let the church say amen!
God is our certain hope in times of trial.
Let the church say amen!
Our God is an awesome God.
Let the church say amen!

PRAISE SENTENCES (MARK 1)
Praise Jesus who calls us!
Praise Jesus who leads us!
Praise Jesus who loves us!
Praise Jesus who saves us!
Praise Jesus!

OPENING PRAYER (MARK 1)
Gracious Christ,
    you came to the fishermen
        when the prophet John was taken away.
Come to us now,
    as we fear losses of our own.

Grant us courage to cast aside
   the nets that bind us,
   to follow you into true freedom
      and newness of life.
Help us to be faithful disciples,
   that we might inspire others
      to follow in your ways. Amen.

OPENING PRAYER (PSALM 62)
Loving God,
   for you alone our souls wait in silence.
You are our shelter in the storm,
   our hope in times of trial.
When our courage falters,
   be our rock and our fortress.
When all hope seems lost,
   lift us up in the arms of your salvation,
   that we might lift up others.
Be our true home, O God,
   that silent place in our souls
   where prayers are answered
      and peace is found. Amen.

PRAYER OF CONFESSION (JONAH 3)
Holy God,
   we would rather proclaim death to our enemies,
   than see them forgiven and redeemed.
Forgive our hardness of heart, O God,
   and our reluctance to see your divine image
   in those who hate and despise us.
Teach us to love our enemies,
   that our lives may proclaim your truth—
   that love is stronger than hate,
and mercy is greater than vengeance.
   We ask this in the name of the Prince of Peace. Amen.

ASSURANCE OF PARDON (JOHN 3, ROMANS 6, ROMANS 8)

Hear the good news: Jesus came to save the world,
not to condemn it.
We who were dead to our sins have been raised
to newness of life through Jesus
who is the Lord of Life.

BENEDICTION (PSALM 62)

God is our rock and our salvation.
We go forth with the blessings of God.
God is our fortress against the storm.
We go forth with the blessings of God.
God is our eternal hope.
We go forth with the blessings of God.

BENEDICTION (MARK 1)

Christ is calling us forth.
**We walk in the footsteps of the disciples
who went before us.**
Christ is calling us forth.
**We go with the blessings of God
who leads us into life.**

JANUARY 29, 2006

Fourth Sunday after the Epiphany

B. J. Beu

COLOR

Green

SCRIPTURE READINGS

Deuteronomy 18:15-20; Psalm 111; 1 Corinthians 8:1-13; Mark 1:21-28

THEME IDEAS

The mighty acts of God are interwoven with the promise to teach God's people the ways of life. In Deuteronomy, the people are so frightened by the immediacy of God's power that they seek guidance through intermediaries, prophets, whom God promises to send. The psalmist proclaims God's faithfulness, not only for our physical needs, but also for our spiritual needs. The idols and lesser gods feared in Deuteronomy are revealed by Paul to be literally nothing. We must be careful with this knowledge, however, lest our actions surrounding these idols cause less mature Christians to stumble in their faith. Finally, the Gospel reading shows Jesus' power over even the unclean spirits. Jesus' teaching comes with such authority and raw power, it appears new.

CALL TO WORSHIP (PSALM 111)
Praise the Lord!
We give thanks to God with all our heart.
The works of the Lord are great
and marvelous in our eyes.
**We delight in God's works
and sing praises to God's name.**
The Lord feeds the faithful, and watches over those
who observe the commandments.
**God's covenant is a blessing.
God's precepts are righteous and just.**
The fear of the Lord is the beginning of wisdom.
Let us worship God and be counted among the wise.

CALL TO WORSHIP (MARK 1)
Listen, Christ is teaching.
We sit at the feet of our teacher.
Listen, the teachings of Christ set the captives free.
We sit at the feet of our teacher.
Listen to Christ's teaching, full of power and authority.
We sit at the feet of our teacher.

CONTEMPORARY GATHERING WORDS (DEUTERONOMY 18)
Where have all the prophets gone?
**They are all around us,
sitting here in our midst.**
What have they to teach us?
**They teach us God's ways,
as they have always done.**
In whose name do they speak?
**They speak in God's name,
and in the name of Jesus Christ.**
How will we know if they speak the truth?
**The Spirit will lead us into truth,
as it has always been.**

CONTEMPORARY GATHERING WORDS (PSALM 111)

Praise the Lord, you people of God.
We have come to sing, and laugh,
and shout God's praises for all to hear!
Listen to the Lord, you people of God.
We have come to hear God's word,
and ponder the mysteries of God's sacred promises.
Praise the Lord, you people of God.
Our God is an awesome God,
greatly to be praised.

PRAISE SENTENCES (PSALM 111)

Praise the Lord!
Delight in God's works!
Praise the Lord!
Rejoice in God's word!
Praise the Lord!
Praise the Lord!
Praise the Lord!

OPENING PRAYER (DEUTERONOMY 18)

Mighty God,
    we long to hear again,
        of your deeds of power and might.
We long to see that pillar of fire
    that led your people
        through the desert wilderness.
We long to hear your voice,
    telling us what to do.
Send us prophets to teach us your ways.
Help us recognize them within our midst,
    that we might hear your words
        in the lessons they teach. Amen.

OPENING (MARK 1)

God of power and might,
  you sent prophets to your people,
    calling us back to your covenant,
    and teaching us your ways.
In the fullness of time,
  you sent us your Son Jesus,
  teaching with such authority,
  that our eyes were opened
    to see your ways anew.
Open our hearts and minds,
  that we may understand
  and proclaim your teachings
    for all to hear.
In Jesus' name we pray. Amen.

BENEDICTION (DEUTERONOMY 18, PSALM 111)

May the God who led us across the wilderness
in a pillar of fire, set our hearts aflame.
  God's righteous love leads us forth.
May the God who gave us the law on Mount Horeb
bless us with understanding and wisdom.
  God's righteous love leads us forth.
May the God who sends us prophets to guide us
continue to lead us into truth.
  God's righteous love leads us forth.

BENEDICTION (PSALM 111)

The works of the Lord sustain us.
  God has blessed us with life.
The precepts of the Lord guide us.
  God has blessed us with wisdom.
The love of the Lord redeems us.
  God has blessed us with salvation.
Go with God's blessings.

FEBRUARY 5, 2006

Fifth Sunday after the Epiphany
Mary J. Scifres

COLOR
Green

SCRIPTURE READINGS
Isaiah 40:21-31; Psalm 147:1-11, 20c; 1 Corinthians 9:16-23; Mark 1:29-39

THEME IDEAS
God's compassion is a central tenet of today's readings. In Isaiah, God's everlasting presence and promise of renewal find poetic expression. In Psalm 147, we praise God for the compassion and healing offered to all who are in need. Paul writes of his call to express the saving love of God to all people—doing all of the ministry he can, with all the people he can, in any way he can. And the healing of Simon's mother-in-law in Mark's Gospel initiates a series of compassionate healings and miracles at the hands of Jesus. In these acts of compassion, the good news is seen and heard so that we may know and hear that Christ is the everlasting God, offering love to the weak and the downtrodden!

CALL TO WORSHIP (PSALM 147)
Come, sing a new song to God.
Praise the One who gathers us here.

Give thanks for the rain, the grass, and the earth.
Give thanks for the gifts of God.
Come, sing a song of praise.
We sing to the everlasting God.

CALL TO WORSHIP (ISAIAH 40)

Do you know? Do you hear?
Our God is from everlasting to everlasting.
Come to know. Come to hear.
Our God gives powers to the weak.
Are you tired? Are you faint?
Our God will renew your strength.
Come, lift up your weary arms.
Rise up like eagles on the wings of God!

CALL TO WORSHIP (ISAIAH 40)

Have you not known?
Have you not heard?
Yahweh is the everlasting God,
    the Creator of all to the ends of the earth.

CALL TO WORSHIP (PSALM 147, ISAIAH 40)

Gather us in, the brokenhearted and the joyful.
Gather us in, the weak and the strong.
Gather us in, the fearful and the brave.
Gather us in, the young and the old.
Gather us in, to sing of God's works.
Gather us in, to praise Jesus Christ.
Gather us in, to worship and wonder.
Gather us in, to know of God's love.

CONTEMPORARY GATHERING WORDS (PSALM 147)

Hallelujah! Sing praise to God!
For God has called us here.
Hallelujah! Sing praise to God!
Let us worship the Lord of life.

PRAISE SENTENCES (PSALM 147)

Praise the Lord! Sing of joy and hope!
Praise the Lord! Sing of joy and hope!
Great is God, and greatly to be praised!
Great is God, and greatly to be praised!

OPENING PRAYER (ISAIAH 40)

Holy One, we come to you,
    listening for your word of compassion.
Renew us with your strength.
Empower us with your love.
Guide us in your ways,
    that we may know you and worship you,
    our everlasting God.

OPENING PRAYER (PSALM 147)

Gracious God,
    hear our songs.
Gather us in as one people,
    that we may worship you as one body.
Heal our broken hearts and bind up our wounds
    that we may come into your presence
        healthy and whole.
As we seek your wisdom.
Help us to discern your greatness,
    as we honor the power and glory of your love.
    Amen.

PRAYER (MARK 1)

O Christ, our healer,
    hear us as we pray.
Heal us in our sickness
    and comfort us in our sorrow.
Impassion us in our apathy
    and strengthen us in our doubt.
Help us to know and accept your healing grace,

that we may rise up and minister amongst your
people.
Help us to go forth,
showing your love
to all who search for you.
Speak through us
that our lives and our words
may proclaim your good news. Amen.

BENEDICTION (ISAIAH 40)
Go forth with the power of God.
Go into the world with the strength of faith.

BENEDICTION (ISAIAH 40)
May you run and not be weary.
May you rise up on the wings of eagles.
May you know without doubt
that the everlasting God goes with you!

BENEDICTION (1 CORINTHIANS 9)
Proclaim the gospel, the promise of hope!
Preach to the world, the truth of God's love.
Do all the good you can, in any way you can,
to all the people you meet!

FEBRUARY 12, 2006

Sixth Sunday after the Epiphany
Erik Alsgaard

COLOR
Green

SCRIPTURE READINGS
2 Kings 5:1-14; Psalm 30; 1 Corinthians 9:24-27; Mark 1:40-45

THEME IDEAS
The theme of today's lectionary readings is healing. From the Old Testament lesson of the healing of Naaman, to the Markan account of the healing of the leper, to the praise and thanksgiving offered in the Psalter, today's scriptures point to the glorious truth that God heals. When focusing on healing, it is tempting to dwell on the physical aspects and the many "why" questions that arise when physical healing does not happen—or at least does not happen the way we want it to (see 2 Kings 5:11). The preacher and worship planner may also wish to search the ways God provides spiritual healing, and/or delve into the ways healing has already occurred in the life of the congregation.

CALL TO WORSHIP (PSALM 30)
I will praise you, O God, for you have lifted me up.
You did not let my foes rejoice over me.
You, O God, have healed me,

You have brought up my soul from the pits of hell.
I will sing and praise you, O God.
I give thanks for your holy name.
You have turned my mourning into dancing.
You have clothed me with joy.
My soul will praise you, O God, and it will not be silent.
O Lord my God, I will give thanks to you forever.

CALL TO WORSHIP (PSALM 30)

All the days of my life, O God,
I have struggled with disease and illness.
But your love remains steadfast.
In my comings and goings, my growing older day by day,
your love remains steadfast.
As the stress of life grows ever greater,
and as the material promises of this world fail one by one,
your love remains steadfast.
In all my weakness, O God,
I have relied on your grace and your love.
O Lord my God, I give thanks to you
for healing and life!

CALL TO WORSHIP (PSALM 30)

Like a person admitted to the emergency room
in need of defibrillation,
you have brought me back from the brink of death,
O God.
Even though cancer seeks to remove my hair, my voice,
my strength, my sense of taste,
nothing can remove your love from me, O God.
In the middle of the night, when all about is quiet
and the only sounds are my anxieties and fears
creeping through my veins,
your love sustains me and brings me
through to the morning.
In the middle of the afternoon, when chaos threatens,

and the priorities of our professions and family
seem mutually exclusive,
   **your love sustains me and brings me
   a sense of purpose and priority.**
Does illness praise you, O God? Does death?
   **No! For you, O God, have removed the bonds
   of sin and death, and I will sing your praises forever.**

CONTEMPORARY GATHERING WORDS (MARK 1)

There are days and times when the only question on our lips
is "why?" Why did my child have to get sick? Why is my
husband suffering with cancer? Why did I get Lupus? For all
the days that end in why, you, O God, are there. I don't have
to know the answers just now. I don't have to understand
everything you are doing. I just have to trust, remain faithful, remain steady, and remain connected to my community
of faith and prayer. I need to remain faithful—even if that
means reaching out when I feel like staying secret; even if
that means telling my best friend that I have a drinking
problem; even if that means telling my prayer circle that my
best friend has breast cancer. Healing is what God desires.
Healing is what God does. Come, see and hear that God's
promises are still real. Come, see and hear that God is alive
and well and living in (the name of your town or church)!

PRAISE SENTENCES

Sing and dance and leap for joy,
   God has brought us safely to this house of worship.
I've got joy, joy, joy, joy, down in my heart,
   and I'm gonna let my face show it today!

OPENING PRAYER (MARK 1)

Gracious and living God,
   we give you thanks for this day
      and for the promises you give us.
Help us live each day

in the fullness of those promises,
that we might experience healing and wholeness
all the days of our lives.
In Jesus' name we pray. Amen.

UNISON PRAYER (PSALM 30)
Like two-year-old children,
we turn to you many times in our lives and ask,
"Why, Lord?"
Often with tears in our eyes and with an anxious heart,
we await your answer.
In those times, help us to trust you more fully,
to cling more tightly to your promises,
and to listen ever more intently
for that still small voice
that seeks to touch us with your love.
In Jesus' name we pray. Amen.

BENEDICTION (MARK 1)
And now may the healing, peace and love of God
the Father, his only Son, our Lord, Jesus Christ,
and the power of the Holy Spirit
be yours this day and forever more. Amen.

BENEDICTION (2 KINGS 5)
God is flat-out in the healing business.
It often doesn't look like what we expect it to be,
but it's there:
when we are able to forgive one another,
when we bring peace and wholeness
to a hurting world,
when we bring newness
to the dead and parched areas of our lives.
See, God makes all things new!
Go forth, in the strength of God's love
and God's promise of love and peace. Amen.

FEBRUARY 19, 2006

Seventh Sunday after the Epiphany
Robert Blezard

COLOR
Green

SCRIPTURE READINGS
Isaiah 43:18-25; Psalm 41; 2 Corinthians 1:18-22; Mark 2:1-12

THEME IDEAS
God's mercy and grace are larger than our sinfulness and tenacious intransigence, and God is eager to do whatever it takes to bring us into righteousness. This theme underlies all of the readings. Isaiah proclaims that God is going to do a new thing for God's people, despite God's weariness with them. In 2 Corinthians, Paul assures us that God's answer is always a "yes," and Mark's Gospel shows Jesus forgiving sins and healing a paralytic. God is eager to forgive and save.

CALL TO WORSHIP (ISAIAH 43)
God has made a way in the wilderness.
We will set our feet on the path of the Lord.
God has brought a river to the desert.
We will drink from God's holy waters.
God is doing a new thing for us.
We will praise God and worship the Lord!

CONTEMPORARY GATHERING WORDS (2 CORINTHIANS 1)

Say "Amen" to the glory of God.
God's word is always "yes."
Proclaim the truth of God's mercy.
In Christ, every one of God's promises is a "yes."
God calls us to worship in holiness.
"Yes!" We answer, "Yes! Yes! Yes!"

CONTEMPORARY GATHERING WORDS (2 CORINTHIANS 1, ISAIAH 43)

What can you count on in this crummy world?
God's promises are always sure.
I'm no good. Why would God care about me?
God forgives everyone. It's God's thing.

PRAISE SENTENCES (ISAIAH 43)

We lift our hearts to you, O holy and ever-living God.
Your mercy overflows our lives.
You make a way through the wilderness to reach us.
You water us with a river through the desert.
You blot out our transgressions and forgive our sins.
We give you thanks and sing your name
    to the ends of the earth.

OPENING PRAYER (ISAIAH 43)

You are doing a new thing with us, O God.
Long is your patience and bottomless your mercy.
You never give up on us
    though we turn away again and again.
In the waters of baptism
    you made us your own
        and freed us from sin and death.
And when we are thirsty,
    locked in the desert of our spirit,

you water us,
  not with a flask,
  but with a river.
Teach us your ways, O God,
  and lead us on your path. Amen.

OPENING PRAYER (MARK 2)

O God of love,
  all of us are imperfect
  and crippled in our sinful natures.
But through your love for us,
  you sent your Son, Jesus Christ,
    to forgive our sins, heal our ills,
    and bring us to new life in you.
We pray your presence here
  will open our hearts to receive the blessings
    you desire for us this day.
In Jesus' name we pray. Amen.

PRAYER OF CONFESSION (ISAIAH 43)

You grow weary with our iniquities, O God.
  We burden you with our sins.
We fail time and again to measure up.
  **We fail to live in ways that would bring honor
  to your name.**
We fail to call your name or sing your praises.
  Have mercy upon us, and forgive us.

WORDS OF ASSURANCE (ISAIAH 43)

Hear the words of the Lord:
  "I will make a way in the wilderness
    and rivers in the desert.
For I give water in the wilderness,
  rivers in the desert, to give drink
    to my chosen people.

I, I am He who blots out your transgressions
  for my own sake,
  and I will not remember your sins."

BENEDICTION (2 CORINTHIANS 1, MARK 2)
Through Christ Jesus,
  every one of God's promises to you is a "Yes."
May God say, "Yes" and heal your deepest hurts,
May God say, "Yes" and forgive all your sins.
And May God say, "Yes" and lead you
  in new ways of living.

BENEDICTION (ISAIAH 43)
May God do a new thing with you,
  make a way in your wilderness
  and cause a river to spring forth
    in the midst of your desert dryness.
May God keep you as a chosen child,
  now and forever.

FEBRUARY 26, 2006

Transfiguration Sunday
B. J. Beu

COLOR
White

SCRIPTURE READINGS
2 Kings 2:1-12; Psalm 50:1-6; 2 Corinthians 4:3-6; Mark 9:2-9

THEME IDEAS
The mystery and wonder shrouding God's holiness is the central theme in today's scripture readings. Just as Elijah was taken up to heaven in a fiery chariot, in a whirlwind shrouded in mystery, so too Jesus was transfigured upon the mountaintop with his disciples. The essence of glory is mystery, and the essence of mystery is wonder.

CALL TO WORSHIP (PSALM 50)
God has summoned us here.
We have come to worship the Lord!
God has summoned us here.
The holiness of God shines forth!
God has summoned us here.
We have come to worship the Lord!

CALL TO WORSHIP (MARK 9)
Behold the Lord, transfigured before us
on the mountaintop.

But we are afraid.
Behold the Lord, standing before us
with robes of dazzling white.
Such power is too great for us.
Behold the Lord, speaking with Moses and Elijah,
the greatest prophets in history.
We long to hear and understand.
Behold the voice of God, proclaiming to us:
"This is my Son, the Beloved. Listen to him."
We have come to listen and believe.

CONTEMPORARY GATHERING WORDS (2 KINGS 2)

The majesty of God is too great for you to bear.
We will not turn back.
The mystery of God is too deep for you to fathom.
We will not turn back.
The fiery chariot of Elijah is beyond your power to see.
We will not turn back.
Come then, and let us worship our God
who took Elijah up to heaven in a whirlwind.
We will worship the Lord our God.

CONTEMPORARY GATHERING WORDS (PSALM 50)

Gather 'round, God is speaking.
God calls to the faithful,
from the rising of the sun to its setting.
Gather 'round, God is speaking.
God's decrees are like a devouring fire,
calling us to repent of all evil.
Gather 'round, God is speaking.
God's precepts resound throughout the earth,
shattering the teachings of the godless.
Gather 'round, God is speaking still.

PPRAISE SENTENCES (MARK 9)

Behold the Man!
Christ is clothed with power and might.
Behold the Man!
Christ is our source of truth and light.
Behold the Man!
Christ is God's beloved Son.
Behold the Man!

OPENING PRAYER (2 KINGS 2, MARK 9)

Everlasting God,
   you come to us shrouded in mystery.
As Elisha sought to follow Elijah to the end,
   we seek to follow Christ up to the mountaintop
      where he was transfigured with Moses and Elijah.
Even when we seek to see you clearly,
our eyes are blinded by the brightness of your glory.
   We long to follow you until the end,
   but are afraid that we might not be up to the journey.
Give us such faith that we too may see the heavens open
   and hear your voice to follow your Son,
      with whom you are well pleased. Amen.

OPENING PRAYER (2 KINGS 2, MARK 9)

God of mystery,
   we come to the mountaintop,
   blinded by the light of your glory.
Like Elisha before us,
   we journey with the hope that our faith will not falter.
We seek answers to questions that have no answers.
Will we see your presence in the whirlwind?
Will we see the fiery chariot connect earth with heaven?
Will we inherent a double portion of the spirit
   of those who went before us?
Will we have the courage even to look up?
Teach us not to fear the unknown.

Help us to embrace those sacred moments
 that shatter our perceptions of power and might.
Open our ears and our hearts to hear your words anew
 to listen to your Son, with whom you are well pleased.
Amen.

BENEDICTION (2 KINGS 2, MARK 9)

May the holy One of Israel,
 the God of our Lord Jesus Christ,
 bless you with a double portion of the Holy Spirit.
May the holy One of Israel open our eyes,
 that we may all see the heavens opened,
 and witness the power connecting heaven and earth
  in the person and work of our Lord, Jesus Christ.
  Amen.

BENEDICTION (2 CORINTHIANS 4)

Go, illuminated by the light of the gospel of Jesus Christ.
 Christ's light shines in the darkness
 and guides us in the knowledge and glory of God.
Go, illuminated by the light of the image of God.
 Christ's light shines in the darkness
 and guides us in the knowledge and glory of God.
Go, illuminated by the light of God's holy love.

MARCH 1, 2006

Ash Wednesday
Bill Hoppe

COLOR

Purple

SCRIPTURE READINGS

Joel 2:1-2, 12-17; Psalm 51:1-17; 2 Corinthians 5:20*b*–6:10;
Matthew 6:1-6, 16-21

THEME IDEAS

Ash Wednesday is the beginning of Lent, the transition
from death to life, and from the darkness and despair of
the Day of the Lord to the light and hope of the Day of
Salvation at Easter. We confront our own frailties and
imperfections as we examine ourselves in the mirror of
these readings. We see the reflection of arrogant hypocrites and hopeless sinners against the light of the Lord,
who is justified in passing judgment. Even on the verge
of certain destruction, *even then,* God reaches out to us
with both hands, calling us to return and to be reconciled. We meet the Lord in that secret place deep within
each of us—our ashen, gray-black hearts—and in this
encounter, our spirits become whiter than snow. We forgive and are forgiven, and begin to understand the extent
of God's relentless affection for all.

CALL TO WORSHIP (JOEL 2, 2 CORINTHIANS 5)
A trumpet sounds from afar . . .
   listen, God is calling!
What does the Lord say to us?
   Now is the time. Today is the day,
Now is the time to return to God!
   Today is the day of our salvation!
Our sins cover us like darkness
spread over the mountains.
   But you, Lord, have shown us your forgiveness.
Praise our God of grace and constant compassion!
   Thanks be to our Lord!

CONTEMPORARY GATHERING WORDS (2 CORINTHIANS 5, 6)
We implore you in Christ's name, and on his behalf.
Be reconciled to God!
The Lord's grace was freely given to us.
Don't let it be in vain!
Though he was innocent,
   it was for our sake that Christ was made one with sin,
   so that we might become one with God's goodness.

PRAISE SENTENCES (2 CORINTHIANS 5)
We are Christ's ambassadors to the world.
God has reconciled the world through Christ!

PRAYER OF CONFESSION (PSALM 51)
Lord, by your grace and mercy, in your pure love,
   wash away our guilt, cleanse us from our sins.
There is no way to hide what we've done.
   Our misdeeds constantly confront us.
We deserve your judgment,
   but we plead for your forgiveness.
You alone can change us and transform us.
   You alone can restore our joy.

Create a pure heart within us, Lord.
Renew us, revive us, and uphold us.
Open our mouths that we might proclaim your praises.
Give us voices to sing of your deliverance! Amen.

OPENING PRAYER (PSALM 51, MATTHEW 6, LENT)

Our hearts are laid bare before you, Lord.
You see us as no one else does.
You see past the impostor's masks that we wear.
O God, we come to worship you—
    not with empty words and meaningless acts of piety,
    but with lonely, aching spirits.
We long for the days of joy and gladness
    that we have known with you.
Fold back the darkness that surrounds us.
Show us your mercy.
Cover us with your grace.
We return our whole hearts to you this day,
    as we pray humbly together in the name of Jesus.
Amen.

PRAYER OF CONFESSION (PSALM 51, MATTHEW 6)

We make a show of our faith and devotion
    on far too many occasions, Lord.
We pride ourselves in our many eloquent
    yet insincere prayers,
    fooling ourselves into believing that you give credence
        to such nonsense.
We forget that you already know our needs
    long before we begin to pray.
We fail to see that we are storing up our treasure on
        earth,
    rather than in heaven.
O God, we earnestly seek your forgiveness.
Help us in our unbelief.

Return us to your secret place
  of divine wisdom and holy mystery,
  the place where you are always ready to meet us,
  the inner chamber of our hearts
    where we can worship you in spirit and truth.
In the name of Jesus we pray. Amen.

WORDS OF ASSURANCE (PSALM 51)
The Lord takes no pleasure in our earthly offerings,
  but delights in the sacrifice of our broken spirits.
God will never turn away a wounded heart.

BENEDICTION (2 CORINTHIANS 6)
Though we were overwhelmed by sorrow,
  in Christ, we can rejoice.
Though we were dead,
  in Christ, we are alive.
Though we have nothing,
  in Christ, we possess everything.
In Christ, the day of deliverance has dawned!
  Amen!

MARCH 5, 2006

First Sunday in Lent
Mary Petrina Boyd

COLOR
Purple

SCRIPTURE READINGS
Genesis 9:8-17; Psalm 25:1-10; 1 Peter 3:18-22; Mark 1:9-15

THEME IDEAS
The waters of grace flow through these scriptures: from God's deliverance of Noah and all animals from the waters of the flood, to the baptism of Jesus in the waters of the Jordan, to our baptisms that bring us salvation. God made a covenant with all creatures in Genesis. The psalmist reminds us that we are to keep our covenant. And, in Jesus Christ, we find a new covenant of water and spirit. This is the good news: God is faithful, merciful, and full of steadfast love; God remembers creation and the everlasting covenant of forgiveness; God has come in Jesus Christ, Beloved Son and Savior of the world. Come back to God, for it is only here that we find true hope, true life, and true joy.

CALL TO WORSHIP (GENESIS 9)
Come, all you people, come and worship.
God has made a covenant with us.
Come, all creatures of the earth, come and worship.

God has made a covenant with all creatures.
Remember the covenant and be thankful.
God remembers the covenant and God will save us.

CALL TO WORSHIP (PSALM 25)

We trust in you, O God, for you are faithful.
Show us your ways and teach us your paths.
We wait for you.
Lead us in your paths of truth.
Do not remember our failures.
Out of your merciful grace, forgive us.
You are faithful, O God. Your love is steadfast.
We lift up our souls to you,
and praise you always.

CALL TO WORSHIP (MARK 1)

John baptized Jesus in the waters of the Jordan.
God said: You are my Son, the Beloved.
With you I am well pleased.
We are washed by the waters of our baptism.
God says: You are my beloved children.
With you I am well pleased.
We gather as God's beloved children
to worship and to serve.
Let us tell the good news of God's love!

CALL TO WORSHIP (1 PETER 3)

Send the waters of your grace upon us.
We are your people.
Let the waters of your love wash us.
We are your forgiven people.
Let the waters of your blessing pour over us.
We are your beloved people.
Thanks be to God.

CALL TO WORSHIP (MARK 1)

We are gathered to worship our God.
Send your Spirit upon us.

We come from many places, with many burdens.
Send you Spirit upon us.
We turn our hearts to you, O God.
Send your Spirit upon us,
and make us your beloved family.

CONTEMPORARY GATHERING WORDS (GENESIS 9, PSALM 25, MARK 1)

God said, "I will be your God."
God has promised. God remembers. God is faithful.
God said, "I will lead you in the paths of truth."
God has promised. God remembers. God is faithful.
God said, "I will forgive you."
God has promised. God remembers. God is faithful.
God said, "My kingdom is near."
God has promised. God remembers. God is faithful.

PRAISE SENTENCES (PSALM 25)

I lift my soul to you, O my God.
I trust in you, O merciful Lord.
You are my God.

PRAISE SENTENCES (GENESIS 9)

God will not fail us.
God remembers us.
We are held in God's love.

PRAISE SENTENCES (GENESIS 9, 1 PETER 3, MARK 1)

God remembers us.
God saves us.
God calls us beloved.

OPENING PRAYER (GENESIS 9, PSALM 25, MARK 1)

God of the covenant,
    you are ever faithful.

Your love never ends.
Teach us your ways.
And guide us in your paths of love and forgiveness,
    that we may witness to your grace
    and salvation. Amen.

OPENING PRAYER (GENESIS 9, PSALM 25, MARK 1)
Faithful God,
    you called all creatures into being,
    and you care for each one.
Send your grace upon your people gathered here,
    that we may follow your ways of truth,
    and walk in the paths of steadfast love,
    proclaiming the good news of Jesus Christ. Amen.

PRAYER OF CONFESSION (GENESIS 9, PSALM 25)
God of the rainbow,
    you made a covenant with all creatures,
    promising life and hope.
God of pathways,
    you show us how we should walk.
Yet we forget our connection with one another
    and think that we are the center of the universe.
We wander from your paths of truth
    into paths of deceit and pride.
Forgive us and lead us back
    into the arms of your love. Amen.

WORDS OF ASSURANCE
God is merciful and full of steadfast love.
God will not forget us.
God will wash us clean,
    and lead us on paths of steadfast love
    and faithfulness.

BENEDICTION (GENESIS 9, PSALM 25, MARK 1)

Walk in the paths of steadfast love and faithfulness.
Dwell under the rainbow of God's love.
Proclaim the good news of God, for God's realm is near.

BENEDICTION (GENESIS 9, PSALM 25, MARK 1)

Go and testify to God's faithful promises.
God's covenant is everlasting.
Go and follow God's ways.
**The ways of the Lord are steadfast love
and faithfulness.**
Go and proclaim God's good news.
The time is now. Turn to God.

BENEDICTION (MARK 1)

We have received the Spirit.
We are blessed by God.
Believe the gospel.
Proclaim the good news.

MARCH 12, 2006

Second Sunday in Lent
Robert Blezard

COLOR
Purple

SCRIPTURE READINGS
Genesis 17:1-7, 15-16; Psalm 22:23-31; Romans 4:13-25; Mark 8:31-38

THEME IDEAS
No matter what our situation or station in life, God calls us to fulfill our purpose in God's plan. Abram was ninety-nine years old when God revealed his place in God's scheme. God deemed Abram a righteous man, as Paul tells us, because of the patriarch's faith. So it is with us. As Paul goes on to say, we are held righteous not because of our works but because of our faith in Christ. This is God's covenant with us, a promise that God will fulfill.

CALL TO WORSHIP (MARK 8)
Let us turn our minds from human things.
Our faith in Jesus saves us.
Let us set our minds on divine things.
Our faith in Jesus saves us.
We will deny ourselves and take up our cross.
Our faith in Jesus saves us.
We will lose all; that we may gain all.
Our faith in Jesus saves us.

CALL TO WORSHIP (ROMANS 4)
Hear of God's promise.
The promise rests on grace.
God gives life to the dead.
The promise rests on grace
God calls into being things that did not exist.
The promise rests on grace.
God came to us through Jesus.
The promise rests on grace.
Jesus died and rose again to save us.
God's grace comes to us through our faith.

CONTEMPORARY GATHERING WORDS (PSALM 22)
God hears when we cry out.
We wail like babies.
God feeds the poor and they are satisfied.
We are hungry.
God is awesome.
Praise God's holy name!

PRAISE SENTENCES (PSALM 22)
All honor and glory to you, O God,
your mercy knows no limit,
and your love knows no depth.
You hold out your hand and the afflicted are healed,
and the poor are fed.
Your benevolence is steadfast,
and your promise is sure
from generation to generation.

OPENING PRAYER (GENESIS 1)
God of Abraham our father, God of Sarah our mother,
we remember with gratitude your covenant
that undergirds our lives with certainty
and gives us peace.

Through the gift of your Son,
you freed us from sin and death.

OPENING PRAYER (MARK 8)
God, you have given us everything.
What can we give in return for our lives?
Be our guide on our Lenten journey.
Help us to deny ourselves,
pick up our cross and follow Jesus.
We welcome the chastening direction in our lives
as we worship you today.

PRAYER OF CONFESSION (MARK 8)
Merciful God,
we confess that our sin turns us from you
again and again.
We are a sinful generation
longing for your mercy.
We want not only to save our lives,
but to gain the whole world as well.
We are too often ashamed to show our faith
to the world around us.
Have mercy on us. Amen.

WORDS OF ASSURANCE (ROMANS 4)
If we rely upon the law of God,
we are beyond hope.
But in God's mercy we are declared righteous
through our faith in Jesus, who died for our sins.

BENEDICTION (PSALM 22)
Go in God's grace.
May peace reign in your hearts forever!

BENEDICTION (GENESIS 17)

God's promises endure from generation to generation.
May the God of Abraham and Sarah,
  the God who sent Jesus to redeem us,
  the God whose covenant is eternal,
  bless you and make you fruitful.

MARCH 19, 2006

Third Sunday in Lent
Jamie Greening

COLOR
Purple

SCRIPTURE READINGS
Exodus 20:1-17; Psalm 19; 1 Corinthians 1:18-25; John 2:13-22

THEME IDEAS
Lenten themes of denial, doctrine, and the dusty wilderness focus these readings upon the coming cross of Christ. The lectionary texts call for additional opportunities of natural revelation, covenant, wisdom, purity, and teachings about the nature of worship. Specific doctrinal issues involve the necessity of preaching, general versus specific revelation, the Ten Commandments, law and gospel, salvation, and sacrifice. Social and contemporary themes could include corruption and abuses within the church, adultery and family issues, environmental concerns, missions, and the Christian message in cultural contexts.

CALL TO WORSHIP (PSALM 19)
Heaven declares your glory.
The church proclaims your glory.
Creation praises you.
Our voices join with nature.

CALL TO WORSHIP (1 CORINTHIANS 1)

Where is the wise person?
She seeks God the Father.
Where is the scholar?
He learns from the Holy Spirit.
Where is the philosopher?
She worships Jesus at the foot of the cross.
The foolishness of God is the wisdom of the ages.

GATHERING WORDS (JOHN 2, LENT)

In this penitent season, we are passionate for your house.
Holy Spirit, examine us by the power of your word,
    the righteousness of your law,
    and the awareness of our sin.

CONTEMPORARY GATHERING WORDS (JOHN 2)

Zeal for your house consumes us.
May this be a place of prayer and peace.

PRAISE SENTENCES (EXODUS 20)

The Lord is the one true God!
We honor our God in Heaven: Father, Son,
    and Holy Spirit.
The Lord is the one true God!
The Spirit guides us in good works.
The Lord is the one true God!
The Son makes atonement for our many sins.
Give glory to the Triune God for ever and ever. Amen.

OPENING PRAYER (PSALM 19)

May the words of my mouth,
    and the meditations of our hearts
        be pleasing and acceptable to you today,
Lord Jesus Christ,
    our rock and redeemer. Amen.

PRAYER OF CONFESSION (EXODUS 20)

Hear the commandments of God:
I am the Lord your God, who brought you
  out of bondage.
You shall have no other gods before me.
Lord, forgive our idolatry.
You shall not make for yourself any idol.
Lord, forgive us for chasing lesser gods.
You shall not misuse the name of the Lord your God.
Lord, forgive our blasphemy.
Remember the Sabbath Day and keep it holy.
Lord, forgive our forgetfulness.
Honor your father and your mother.
Lord, forgive us for neglecting our elders.
You shall not murder.
Lord, forgive us for celebrating violence.
You shall not commit adultery.
Lord, forgive our lustful hearts.
You shall not steal.
Lord, forgive us for oppressing the poor.
You shall not be a false witness.
Lord, forgive our lying lips.
You shall not covet.
Lord, forgive our greedy hearts.
This is the Word of the Lord.
Lord have mercy.
Christ have mercy.
Lord have mercy.

BENEDICTION (1 CORINTHIANS 1)

Let us live in the wisdom of God.
May we leave in the power of the cross.

We depart to serve in a perishing world.
Let us live in the wisdom of God.

BENEDICTION
May the promises of the Lord
and the nearness of God's Spirit
draw you all closer to Christ.

MARCH 26, 2006

Fourth Sunday in Lent
One Great Hour of Sharing
Sara Dunning Lambert

COLOR
Purple

SCRIPTURE READINGS
Numbers 21:4-9; Psalm 107:1-3, 17-22; Ephesians 2:1-10; John 3:14-21

THEME IDEAS
Throughout these scriptures, we learn of God's saving grace. God listens to the cries of God's people in the wilderness. Through Moses, God provides a symbol of forgiveness and healing, in the form of a bronze serpent on a pole. John recalls this incident, comparing Jesus on the cross as our symbol of forgiveness, given in love for the whole world. The psalmist reminds us that God delivered those who cried out in their pain, and Paul describes God as rich in mercy, despite our sins.

CALL TO WORSHIP (PSALM 107)
O give thanks to the Lord, for God is good.
God's steadfast love endures forever.
God hears as we cry out in pain, in slavery,
and in despair.

God's faithfulness sustains us through our trials.
With thanksgiving, we praise God's holy name,
the author of our deliverance.
We tell of God's deeds with songs of joy.
O give thanks to the Lord, for God is good.
God's steadfast love endures forever.

CALL TO WORSHIP (JOHN 3, EPHESIANS 2)

God's love for our world is so great,
God sent Christ as a blessing for us all.
God loves us. We share that love with joy!
Everyone who believes in Christ will never perish
but will have eternal life.
We live forever with Christ!
God has not abandoned us to the darkness of night,
but has blessed us with light.
Jesus is the light of the world!
God is rich in mercy.
God's great love brings us life with Christ.
God's mercy is forever! Amen!

CONTEMPORARY GATHERING WORDS (PSALM 107)

We come as we are today, singing our faith.
O give thanks to the Lord, for God is good!
We come as we are today, crying in pain.
O give thanks to the Lord, for God is good!
We come as we are today, full of love.
O give thanks to the Lord, for God is good!
We come as we are today, ready to praise.
O give thanks to the Lord, for God is good!

PRAISE SENTENCES (PSALM 107, JOHN 3, EPHESIANS 2)

The steadfast love of the Lord endures forever!
O give thanks to the Lord, for God is good.

Although we are sick in our hearts,
  we know God's forgiveness comes.
God listens to our prayers and responds.
God loved us so much he sent Jesus to be our light
  and our Savior.
God is rich in mercy and forgiveness!

OPENING PRAYER (NUMBERS 21, JOHN 3, LENT)

Merciful Lord,
  we ask for your presence with us this morning,
  as we contemplate our Lenten journey
    through the wilderness of this world.
As Moses gave the Hebrew people
  your symbol of forgiveness and healing,
  give to us your symbol of forgiveness and grace—
    your Son Jesus Christ.
May we be mindful of your love forever. Amen.

OPENING PRAYER (NUMBERS 21, PSALM 107)

We bask in the healing of your love today, O Lord.
You are with us when we cry out in fear.
You are with us when we are sick with shame.
You are with us when we love each other.
You are with us in your only Son, Jesus.
Carry us through the desert night,
  to the light of your new dawn. Amen.

PRAYER OF CONFESSION (NUMBERS 21)

Holy One,
  in times of need,
  help us to look to you for sustenance.
We weep in our pain and sorrow,
  and in our separateness, hate, and fear.
We are often sick in spirit, mind and body.
We wander in our own wilderness, bitten by snakes,
  tethered to feelings of inadequacy and hopelessness.

Yet you are always with us.
Despite our fragile faith,
    we are assured of your healing love,
    time after time.
By your grace, we are given a symbol of that love—
    your Son, our Savior.
We seek the strength of hope,
    knowing your open arms
        will guide us on our journey. Amen.

BENEDICTION (JOHN 3)

Go forth to serve God in faith, in grace and in mercy.
For God so loved us that he gave us his Son.
Because we believe, we share God's love—
    through the works of our hands, the joy of our hearts,
    and the words of our mouths.

BENEDICTION (PSALM 107, EPHESIANS 2)

God's love lasts forever!
Whatever our pain, whatever our sorrow,
    whatever our faults, God's love is still there for us!
May the peace of God's grace and mercy
    remain in your hearts always. Amen.

APRIL 2, 2006

Fifth Sunday in Lent

Jamie Greening

COLOR
Purple

SCRIPTURE READINGS
Jeremiah 31:31-34; Psalm 51:1-12; Hebrews 5:5-10; John 2:20-33

THEME IDEAS
Traditional Lenten themes of fasting, wilderness, sin, confession, denial, forgiveness, and preparation are appropriate, as this is the last Sunday before the festal days of Palm Sunday and Easter. Textual themes include the importance of covenant, the Word of God, the priesthood of Christ, prayer, sorrow, the crucifixion, and the pain of death. Doctrinal themes could include salvation, the Holy Spirit, the intercessory work of Christ, the victory of Christ over evil, the deity of Christ and atonement. The church models Christ's intercessory ministry for the world. The new covenant in Christ brings awareness and conviction of personal and corporate sin. Confession and repentance lead to praise and thanksgiving. While the mood on this day should be hopeful, yet contemplative and introspective, avoid the temptation to rush to Easter's resurrection.

CALL TO WORSHIP OR PRAYER OF CONFESSION (PSALM 51)

Lord, have mercy.
We come with broken hearts.
We know our transgressions.
Christ, have mercy.
Create in us clean hearts.
Lord, have mercy.
Restore the joy of our salvation.

CALL TO WORSHIP (JEREMIAH 31)

Write your law in our hearts.
You are our God.
Teach us, Lord, to know you better.
Holy Spirit, illumine our minds.
Remember our sins no more.
Christ Jesus, purify us in your new covenant.
By our lives let all humanity know your salvation.

CALL TO WORSHIP (LENT)

Lord, we gather in your presence
  with souls hungry from our Lenten fast.
In the midst of our wilderness,
  we yearn for refreshment
  through your healing and nurturing Holy Spirit.
We are desperate to experience you
  in fresh and new ways.
Prepare our hearts to worship you
  and to receive your word,
  in the name and power of Jesus Christ
  and to the glory of his name.

CONTEMPORARY GATHERING WORDS (PSALM 51, HEBREWS 5)

Let us come before Christ our Lord
  with open and seeking hearts.

We desire purity.
Purify us by your precious Holy Spirit.
**In prayer and praise, we worship Christ Jesus,
our Great High Priest.**

CONTEMPORARY GATHERING WORDS (PSALM 51)

Purify our hearts and gather us into your presence.
Purify our hearts. Create us anew!
Cleanse our minds, and gather us into your grace.
Purify our hearts. Create us anew!
Wash away our sins, and gather us into your holiness.
Purify our hearts. Create us anew!

PRAISE SENTENCES (JOHN 12, HEBREWS 5)

Jesus, you came to glorify God
through your perfect sacrifice.
In being lifted up, you draw all people to yourself,
as the sure source of God's salvation.
We celebrate you now, and rejoice in our redemption.

PRAISE SENTENCES (JEREMIAH 31)

Lord Jesus you are our new covenant.
We, who believe, are the new house of Israel,
and we praise your Holy Name.
We lift up your praises because of your compassion
and mercy toward sinners such as us.

PRAISE SENTENCES (JEREMIAH 31)

The days are coming and surely are here.
God's love is with us now!
The days are coming and surely are here.
God's love is with us now!

PRAISE SENTENCES (JOHN 12)

Glorify the Lord!
Give Christ the glory!

Glorify the Lord
Give Christ the glory now!

OPENING PRAYER (HEBREWS 5)

Heavenly Father,
like Jesus our Lord,
we offer up to you our prayers and petitions
because you alone can save us.
As we gather here to worship,
we ask that by the power and presence of the Holy
Spirit,
we be motivated, convicted, and changed
from the inside out. Amen.

OPENING PRAYER (JOHN 12)

Merciful God,
Good Friday's cross looms ever closer
in our minds and hearts.
Grant us an awareness of our sin,
that we may revel in the atonement
offered to us in Jesus.
May his holy and eternal sacrifice
urge us on to greater faith. Amen.

PRAYER OF CONFESSION (HEBREWS 5)

Jesus offered prayers for God's people,
so do we.
With cries and petitions
we call out to you in the midst of our hurting.
In the agony of our pain
we reach for you.
In the turmoil of our brokenness,
we plead for your healing touch.
Save us God.
Save us from: *(say slowly)*
death, illness, pain, depression, economic oppression,

racial inequity, fear, loneliness, violence, and hate.
We accept your grace
   and providential care for us
   in every area of life
   and cling to your assurance
      of love and acceptance.
In the name of Jesus Christ, our Lord. Amen.

BENEDICTION (PSALM 51)

In your good pleasure Lord, make Zion prosper.
Build up the walls of Jerusalem.
Bless our sacrifices,
   that we may leave in peace.

BENEDICTION (JEREMIAH 31)

Forgive us Lord, for our wickedness.
Remember our sins no more.
As we leave, let us rejoice,
   in the awareness of you.

APRIL 9, 2006

Passion/Palm Sunday
Mary J. Scifres

COLOR
Purple

PALM SUNDAY READINGS
Psalm 118:1-2, 19-29; Mark 11:1-11

PASSION SUNDAY READINGS
Isaiah 50:4-9a; Psalm 31:9-16; Philippians 2:5-11; Mark 14:1–15:47 or Mark 15:1-39 (40-47)

THEME IDEAS
Today's contrasting moods of festivity and solemnity may feel like a conflict of interest. Following the flow of Mark's gospel, worship can move from a time of celebration, as the triumphant entry into Jerusalem is recounted, into a time of reflection and grief, as the trial and death of Jesus are remembered. Throughout the readings, obedience and purpose arise as values that Jesus held dearly, even to the point of facing his own death. As we reflect on Jesus' values and the disciples' response of denial and betrayal, we are challenged to let the mind of Christ guide our lives and our journeys of faith.

OPENING WORDS (PALM SUNDAY, PASSION SUNDAY, MARK 11)

Let us wave palms,
for today we welcome Christ into our midst.
Hosanna to the blessed child of God!
Let us shed tears, for today we remember Jesus' death.
Hosanna to the blessed child of God!
On this day, we bring our palms
and reflect upon Christ's passion.
Hosanna to the blessed child of God!
On this day, we laugh with joy and cry with anguish.
Hosanna to the blessed child of God!
On this day, we begin the holiest week of all.
Hosanna to the blessed child of God!
On this day, we begin to grieve.
So when we celebrate Sunday next week,
we may laugh in the face of anguish,
and celebrate the resurrection of Christ!
Hosanna to the blessed child of God!

CALL TO WORSHIP (PSALM 118, MARK 15)

Today is God's gift, a day made for us.
We rejoice with glad hearts of praise!
Today is Christ's day, a day made for thanks.
We rejoice with glad hearts of praise!
Today, we gather in joy and thanksgiving,
in sorrow and grief, remembering Christ's gift
of great love.
We give thanks for the gift and remember the price,
as we bring our worship to God.

CALL TO WORSHIP (PHILIPPIANS 2)

Let the mind of Christ center our thoughts
and call us to worship.
For the great love of God welcomes us here.

CONTEMPORARY GATHERING WORDS (MARK 11)
Give thanks to God who welcomes us here.
Hosanna in the highest!
Remember Christ who calls us here.
Hosanna in the highest!
Praise the Spirit who fills us here.
Hosanna in the highest!

PRAISE SENTENCES (MARK 11, PSALM 118)
Praise to Jesus the Christ!
Blessed is the One who comes in the name of the Lord!
Praise to Jesus the Christ!
Blessed is the One who comes in the name of the Lord!

OPENING PRAYER (MARK 11, PHILIPPIANS 2, MARK 15)
God of Passion and Palms,
    come to us this day.
Enter into our hearts
    as you once entered into Jerusalem,
    full of passion and purpose.
Help us to receive you with joy and thanksgiving,
    that we may enter into your ministry
        with that same passion and purpose.
Instill in each of us the mind of Christ,
    that we may be your disciples on this earth.
Strengthen our resolve
    when faced with fear and tragedy,
    that we may proclaim your name
        and follow where you lead.
In the name of Christ our Cornerstone, we pray. Amen.

PRAYER OF CONFESSION (PSALM 118, PSALM 31)
Gracious God,
    hear us as we bring our sorrows
        and our fears to you.

Forgive us,
  as we place our sins
    upon the altar of your grace.
Deliver us from the grief that overwhelms us
  and the temptations that call to us.
As we place our trust in your loving strength,
  let your face shine upon us
    and your grace flow within us.
Save us with your steadfast love.
In hope and gratitude, we pray. Amen.

WORDS OF ASSURANCE (PSALM 118)
O give thanks to God above,
  for Christ our Savior is good!
The steadfast love of our God endures forever.
And the grace of our Savior
  overcomes every sin and sorrow.
In the name of Jesus Christ, we are forgiven!

BENEDICTION (PHILIPPIANS 2)
May the mind of Christ rule in your hearts
  and bless your lives.
May the love of Christ bring you joy!

BENEDICTION (MARK 15)
The tomb has been closed, and the stone is shut tight.
What then shall we say?
Christ has died. But Christ will arise.
Christ will come again!

APRIL 13, 2006

Holy Thursday
Bill Hoppe

COLOR
Purple

SCRIPTURE READINGS
Exodus 12:1-4 (5-10), 11-14; Psalm 116:1-4, 12-19;
1 Corinthians 11:23-26; John 13:1-17, 31*b*-35

THEME IDEAS
It was by the blood of a sacrificial lamb that the Hebrews were saved in Egypt, as God passed over their homes. And it was at his final Passover feast that Jesus ate his last meal on earth, showing himself to be the sacrificial Lamb of God, by whose blood the entire world is saved. This was a Passover feast unlike any other. Jesus changed its imagery forever by asking his disciples to eat his body, with the breaking of the bread, and to drink his blood with the sharing of the cup. And so, this meal became for us the Lord's Supper, commemorated as the sacrament of Holy Communion. As doubtful and confused as the disciples must have been, Jesus left no doubt about his love for them, as he washed their feet—even the feet of Judas Iscariot, his betrayer. Sacrifice and love, then, are the foremost themes of Holy Thursday: "Just as I have loved you, you also should love one another" (John 13:34*b*).

CALL TO WORSHIP (JOHN 13, 1 CORINTHIANS 11, EXODUS 12)

A table is set before us. A feast is prepared for us.
A meal of bread and wine, of meat and bitter herbs.
The Lord calls us to this supper of remembrance.
The Lord calls us to serve and to be served.
As we break the bread and share the cup,
our understanding may fail us.
But we will never forget Christ's example.
We will never forget the full extent of his love.

CONTEMPORARY GATHERING WORDS (JOHN 13)

Christ's love is poured out for us
like water poured into a basin.
Christ's love washes us clean.
Christ's love shows us who we are to be,
and what we are to do.
How blessed we are to know such love!

CONTEMPORARY GATHERING WORDS (JOHN 13)

God invites us to the table.
All are welcome, even those with their own agenda.
Christ serves us at this meal.
All may partake, even those who feel unworthy.
All are welcome; all are served; all are loved.

OPENING PRAYER (PSALM 116)

We love you, Lord. You hear us.
You listen to our prayers.
You have always heard us
whenever we've called to you.
Though death tries to bind us
and the gates of hell open before us,
we will call on the Lord's name for deliverance.
You are full of grace and righteousness.
Lord, you are full of compassion!

You have saved us and preserved us, God.
We rest in your love and care.
How can we repay you, Lord,
for the gifts you've showered upon us?
We offer our thanksgiving to you
before all your people!
O praise the Lord!
Praise be to God! Amen.

OPENING PRAYER OR INIVTATION TO COMMUNION (1 CORINTHIANS 11)

On the night of his arrest,
the Lord Jesus took bread and broke it, saying:
"This is my body, given for you. Remember me."
As Jesus gave thanks to God,
we also give thanks for his sacrifice.
On that same night, in the same way,
the Lord Jesus took the cup, saying:
"This is my blood, poured out for you. Remember me."
As Jesus gave thanks to God,
we also give thanks for this new covenant.
When you eat this bread and drink this cup,
remember the Lord Jesus. Remember and be thankful.
Remember until he comes!
Remember us when you come, Lord Jesus!
Thanks be to God!

PRAYER OF CONFESSION (JOHN 13)

Loving Christ,
on that night long ago,
you knew that your hour had come.
You knew full well what lay ahead of you.
Your disciples loved you and followed you,
but they had also failed you.
They would fail you yet again that night,
and one would betray you.

Yet you washed their feet, as a servant would—
even the feet of your betrayer.
We have also loved you and followed you.
We have also failed you,
and we cannot comprehend the love that you show us,
the love that is our example,
the love that tells us to do
as you have done for us.
May we be like you, Master, servants of all.
May all see how we long to be your faithful disciples.
May all see how we love each other,
just as you have loved us.
In your holy name we pray. Amen.

WORDS OF ASSURANCE (JOHN 13)
Now the Son of Man, the one who loves us, is glorified.
In him, God is also glorified.
The one who loves us gives us a new commandment:
to love one another!
As the Lord has loved us, you are to love each other.
Let all see this love among you, and glorify God.
Let all see how you belong to Christ!

BENEDICTION (PSALM 116, JOHN 13)
How precious to the Lord is the death of his faithful ones.
How precious is the sacrifice of Christ.
You are the treasure for which everything was given.
Know that you are precious to God.
And know that you are worthy of Christ's sacrifice.

APRIL 14, 2006

Good Friday

John A. Brewer

COLOR

Black or None

SCRIPTURE READINGS

Isaiah 52:13–53:12; Psalm 22; Hebrews 10:16-25; John 18:1–19:42

THEME IDEAS

"Undying love." Today is the day when this overused cliché holds concrete truth for the followers of Christ. While it wasn't as evident to those who stood beneath the cross on that Friday we call "good," it is clear to us today. In the death of Christ, there is evidence of the undying love of God. A search of the true disciple's heart will reveal the branding of God's redeeming love. Christ was forsaken for love's sake. Such love is for our benefit, calling us to draw near to the throne of God's grace. This sacrificial love is unrelenting, irresistible, never ending, and undying. We will not be forsaken. God enters humanity and dies. God's undying love in Christ is both universal and specific—it is a love for humanity in general and for each individual in particular.

CALL TO WORSHIP (PSALM 22)

All the ends of the earth will remember
and turn to the Lord.

**All the families of the nations
will bow down before God.**
For dominion belongs to the Lord.
God rules over the nations.
**All peoples on the earth will feast and worship.
Those who cannot keep themselves alive
will kneel before the Lord.**
Posterity will serve God.
Future generations will be told about the Lord.
**They will proclaim God's righteousness
to a people yet unborn.**

CALL TO WORSHIP (HEBREWS 10)

This is the covenant I will make with them, says the Lord.
**I will put my laws in their hearts
and I will write them on their minds.**
Let us draw near to God with a sincere heart,
in full assurance of faith.
**Let us hold unswervingly to the hope we profess,
for the One who promised is faithful.**
Let us consider how we may spur one another on
toward love and good deeds.
**Let us not give up meeting together
as some are in the habit of doing.
But let us encourage one another,
as we see the Day of the Lord approaching.**

CALL TO WORSHIP (JOHN 18, JOHN 19)

Come, let us gather again in the shadow
of the Cross of Christ.
**We gather to remember the overwhelming evidence
of Love's ultimate sacrifice.**
Who would have guessed that the height and depth,
the length and width of God's love might look like this:
a forsaken savior on a cross?
Certainly not us. Not us, who are too often lost

amid the world's distractions and responsibilities.
Not us, for whom such love was offered without cost.
Let us gather again in the shadow of the Cross of Christ
and commit ourselves to remember the price paid.
Let us live our lives in a way that indicates why
this Friday is called "Good."
**Thanks be to God, who opened the gates of heaven,
that we might have the faith, hope, and love,
witnessed in Christ's sacrifice for our salvation.**

CONTEMPORARY GATHERING WORDS, (REFERENCING CHARLES WESLEY'S HYMN "AND CAN IT BE THAT I SHOULD GAIN")

Who is the victim of this terrible thing?!
Who is the scapegoat of this horrific thing?!
An innocent man has been ruthlessly killed.
An innocent man has been senselessly sacrificed.
For whom has this man been sacrificed?
For whom has this man been slain as an offering?
For a guilty man he has been hung on a cross.
For a guilty woman he has been pierced.
What kind of man is this?
Who would die in the place of the guilty?
What kind of man is this?
Who would suffer for one who has done evil?
Amazing Love! How can it be
that Thou, my God would die for me?
Amazing Love! How can it be,
that Thou, my Christ would die for me?

PRAISE SENTENCES (HEBREWS 10)

Thanks be to God, who remembers our sins
and our lawless deeds no more.
Thanks be to God, whose forgiveness is now sure
and who no longer demands any offering for sin.
Praise be to God, who has removed the veil,

drawing us near to the throne of grace and mercy.
Let us honor and glorify God, by gathering together
and encouraging us to love one another,
as Christ has loved us.
Praise be to God!

OPENING PRAYER (JOHN 18, JOHN 19, GOOD FRIDAY)

O God of infinite love and power,
we gather together on this Good Friday
to reflect on the passion of the Christ.
We are utterly humbled
in the presence of such love and mercy.
Open our hearts this day
to the goodness of Good Friday,
and fill us with your love
and powerful Spirit of Holiness.
Remove from us all sin.
Offer us anew this Life in Christ
that makes all things new. Amen.

OPENING PRAYER (PSALM 8, HEBREWS 2, GOOD FRIDAY)

O Lord, our Lord,
how majestic is your name in all the earth!
Who are we that you are mindful of us?
Yet, you consider us only a little lower
than the heavenly angels.
O Lord, our Lord,
how majestic is your name in all the earth!
We who need you desperately each day,
have come to you on this Good Friday
to acknowledge the endless love
you have demonstrated on the Cross of Christ.
Inspire us to live each and every day,
in the fullness of your eternal life.

In the name of the love incarnate,
Jesus Christ our Lord. Amen.

UNISON PRAYER OR PRAYER OF CONFESSION (ISAIAH 53, PSALM 51)

We all, like sheep, have gone astray.
We have all turned to our own way.
We have sinned and have been the cause
  of Christ's suffering.
Please forgive us, we pray.
Remove the sins that distance us from you
  and from those we love and care about.
Remove our selfishness, our pride, our envy,
  and our greed.
Remove from us our thoughtless acts
  and words that hurt one another.
Remove from us the tendency to hurt others
  out of revenge and anger.
Forgive us please.
Create in us a clean heart, O Lord.
And renew in us a right spirit. Amen.

WORDS OF ASSURANCE (HEBREWS 10, JEREMIAH 31)

In the name of the compassionate Christ,
  you are forgiven.
For God has declared, "I forgive your evil ways
  and remember your sins no more!"

BENEDICTION (HEBREWS 10)

May you leave this place with the assurance
  of forgiveness that is made possible
    through the sacrifice of Christ.
Go forth in hope and anticipation
  of the ultimate victory that comes with Easter.
Go forth! Be Easter people!

BENEDICTION (1 PETER 2, GOOD FRIDAY)

By his stripes we are healed.
By his wounds, we are made whole.
Go in the name of Jesus Christ
    and live in the salvation made possible
    by the Goodness of this Friday. Amen.

APRIL 16, 2006

Easter Sunday

Joanne Carlson Brown

COLOR
White

SCRIPTURE READINGS
Acts 10:34-43; Psalm 118:1-2, 14-24; 1 Corinthians 15:1-11; John 20:1-18 or Mark 16:1-8

THEME IDEAS
Resurrection—new life! This is the heart of the Christian message and what we are called to witness to at all times. On this glorious feast day, we celebrate God's steadfast love, God conquering fear and death, and the fact that this message is for everyone. With Paul and Peter, this day is a chance to affirm the basis of our beliefs. We need also to recover that sense of grief and despair that brings Mary to the garden in order to fully understand and participate in the astonishment and joy at finding her beloved, risen from the dead. This possibility of encountering the Risen Christ is there for all of us to experience. It is this active, risen presence that needs to come through our liturgies for today.

CALL TO WORSHIP (JOHN 20)
Out of the darkness of grief and despair
comes a message of hope. Christ is risen.

Christ is risen, indeed.
We run to the tomb to see for ourselves.
And it is true. Christ is risen.
Christ is risen, indeed.
We hear a voice call our name,
and we know our risen Lord
is with us now and always.
Christ is risen.
Christ is risen, indeed.
Thanks be to God.

CALL TO WORSHIP (PSALM 118)
Come, give thanks to our God.
God's steadfast love endures forever.
God is our strength and might and salvation.
God's steadfast love endures forever.
Because of this love, we shall not die.
This is God's doing, and it is marvelous in our eyes.
This is the day that our God has made,
let us rejoice and be glad in it.

CALL TO WORSHIP (ACTS 10)
We have a message to preach to all.
Christ is risen.
Christ lived and preached love and liberation among us.
We are witnesses to his mighty acts.
Christ rose from the dead and appears to us still.
We rejoice in the living Savior.
Come; let us worship the God of love and life.

CONTEMPORARY GATHERING WORDS (JOHN 20, EASTER)
Why have you come this morning?
We come to experience the Risen Christ.
How will you know him?
Through the love and life we feel present

in this gathering of the Body of Christ.
What will you do with this experience?
We will go forth, witnesses to this amazing act of love.
Come, then, people of God, let us worship our Easter God.

PRAISE SENTENCES (PSALM 118)

This is the day that the Lord has made,
let us rejoice and be glad in it!
Praise the God of this day,
whose steadfast love endures forever.
Praise the God of salvation who does marvelous things.
Praise the God of everlasting life.

OPENING PRAYER (JOHN 20, EASTER)

O God of all our days,
we come this morning with eager anticipation.
We seek to know you, to see you, to touch you.
Open our hearts,
that we might experience you anew.
Open our lives,
that we may be faithful witnesses
to your resurrection.
May we, with shouts of joy,
proclaim your steadfast, liberating love
to all people, everywhere. Amen.

OPENING PRAYER (JOHN 20, EASTER)

O God,
bless us this morning with resurrection rampage—
a rampage that summons us to shout yes
to the birth of new creation in our midst.
May we experience the birthquakes of new life
in our lives and in our congregation.
The Son is up!
And we are up with the Son,
despite all those things

that seek to pull us down to despair.
We are your Easter people. Amen.

UNISON PRAYER (EASTER)

O God of Easter joy,
we come this morning
with glad shouts of acclamation.
Christ is risen.
Christ is risen, indeed.
May this time of worship
help us to truly and fully experience this Risen Christ.
May we be transformed—
transformed into your butterfly people,
winging through the earth
with messages of beauty, hope and life.
Amen.

BENEDICTION (JOHN 20)

Go forth as God's chosen witnesses,
to proclaim all you have heard and seen and experienced.
We go forth in the name of the Risen Christ.
Go forth sustained by God's steadfast love.
We go forth transformed and transforming.
Go forth with shouts of joy.
Christ is risen, indeed.

BENEDICTION (JOHN 20)

We have come from darkness and despair
to hope and joy.
We have been transformed by new life.
Go forth to witness and to testify to the message of hope
we have received this day.
Christ is risen. Christ is risen indeed. Alleluia.
Amen.

APRIL 23, 2006

Second Sunday of Easter
Judy Schultz

COLOR
White

SCRIPTURE READINGS
Acts 4:32-35; Psalm 133; 1 John 1:1–2:2; John 20:19-31

THEME IDEAS
The reading from Acts gives the biblical basis for communal living, sharing from our abundance and distributing that abundance according to one's individual need. How would our congregations be different if we followed this example of the early church? The reading from the Fourth Gospel, recalling the doubts of Thomas and the demand for tangible proof of the Resurrection, confronts the church with some other questions. How are we to convince those who have never seen Jesus Christ that he lives? If *we* are the Body of Christ, must we also bear the marks of crucifixion? What is the difference between faithful and skeptical doubting? And from the epistle, what does it mean to "walk in the light"? (1 John 7).

CALL TO WORSHIP (PSALM 133)
Come, Easter people, let us worship in unity!
It is good and pleasant to worship God together.
It is as good as the feeling of precious and holy oil,

flowing freely down our face and over our collar.
It is like dew falling freshly on grass,
or snow falling gently on great mountains.
For these are signs that God has ordained blessing
and life forevermore!
We worship God with great joy!

CALL TO WORSHIP (ACTS 4, 1 JOHN 1, JOHN 20)

Come into this fellowship!
Come now into the light!
We come with joy, because we want to walk
in the light of God's grace and truth.
Here is the celebration of great grace.
God has blessed the church with grace
since the resurrection of Jesus.
We come with confidence.
We do not doubt, but we believe.
Then let us worship God together.

CONTEMPORARY GATHERING WORDS (1 JOHN 1, JOHN 20)

Come, people of light!
Come into the light of God's love and power.
Come, people of God's love.
Come into the presence of holy love.
Come, people of truth!
Come in to worship the true God.

PRAISE SENTENCES (1 JOHN 1, EASTER)

We praise you, holy God of Light,
for vanquishing every darkness.
We praise you, Holy Son of God,
for bringing us victory and peace.
We praise you, Holy Spirit,
for filling us with Resurrection power.

OPENING PRAYER (JOHN 20)

Come, O Risen Christ, into our fearful hearts,
and speak again to us your word of peace.
We still fear lesser authorities,
and still worship in secret and doubt.
Come to us. Send us your Spirit. Allay our fears.
Calm our beating hearts, and bring peace
to our warring inclinations,
that we may experience the truth of your life
among us this day. Amen.

OPENING PRAYER OR PRAYER OF CONFESSION (1 JOHN 1)

We come into your presence, O God,
knowing that we have sinned,
yet trusting that if we confess to you,
your forgiveness will be as rain on our gardens,
as sunshine through our kitchen windows,
as smiles on the faces of our friends.
Accept us as we are,
but heal our brokenness.
Forgive our foolishness and self-centeredness.
By the power of your holy love,
make us fit to proclaim your truth,
and strengthened to live in your light. Amen.

UNISON PRAYER OR PRAYER OF CONFESSION (JOHN 20)

Holy Spirit of power and peace,
you have entrusted to us, your church,
the power to forgive sins.
Forgive us, we pray,
when we are slow to forgive,
long-lasting in our grudges,
possessive of our grievances against one another,
and stubborn in our willingness to trust

that your grace enfolds us all
in your holy and unconditional love.
Open our hearts,
as your Risen Son opened the locked door
sheltering his terrified disciples.
And enter fully into us,
that we will be filled with a deep desire
to reconcile and forgive and love one another.
In the name of your Son Jesus, we pray. Amen.

WORDS OF ASSURANCE (1 JOHN 2)
Anyone who sins has an advocate with God:
Jesus Christ, the Son of God.
By his life, death, and resurrection,
he has convincingly demonstrated
that we are never beyond the reach of God's love.
In the name of Jesus,
I proclaim to you, your sins are forgiven!

BENEDICTION (JOHN 20, EASTER)
When you go from here, do not be afraid
to proclaim Jesus' resurrection.
We are sometimes afraid to share our faith,
knowing that other people believe different things.
Live your faith boldly, not giving in to fears,
and be generous with what you can share with others.
We go; convinced that God's love empowers
our generosity. We go; convinced that our lives
can indeed witness to our faith.
Go in peace. Amen.
Amen.

BENEDICTION (ACTS 4, 1 JOHN 1)
Go out from here, and keep walking in the light
of God's truth and love.
From this worshiping fellowship,

we will seek to walk in the light.
Invite others to join you on your journey.
Do not be afraid of the dark.
We will invite others to share our journey
even as we will share ourselves and our goods
with those who are needy.
Go, people of God, and witness to the living Christ
in the world.
We go with joy and peace.

APRIL 30, 2006

Third Sunday of Easter

B. J. Beu

COLOR
White

SCRIPTURE READINGS
Acts 3:12-19; Psalm 4; 1 John 3:1-7; Luke 24:36b-48

THEME IDEAS
The themes of despair and hope, together with death and life, are intermingled in today's scriptures. In Acts, Peter admonishes the crowd for being amazed when Christ's disciples perform works of miraculous healing. Such power comes from the God of Abraham, Isaac, and Jacob—the same God who raised Jesus from the dead. The psalmist calls out with hope in the midst of distress, for in God hope can always be found. The epistle speaks of the hope that comes from being in Christ, and being known by God, even as Christ is known. Finally, the gospel beseeches us to have hope in the face of death, for God is greater than death, and the Messiah's sufferings brought forgiveness of sins and newness of life to those who believe.

CALL TO WORSHIP (ACTS 3)
In the God of Abraham and Sarah there is Life.
The Holy One of God is raised!

In the God of Isaac and Rebecca there is Life.
The Holy One of God is raised!
In the God of Jacob and Rachel there is Life.
The Holy One of God is raised!

CALL TO WORSHIP (LUKE 24)

In the midst of our sorrow and grief,
Christ comes to ease our pain.
In the midst of our doubts and fears,
Christ comes to bring us hope.
In the midst of our sickness unto death,
Christ comes to bring us life.

CONTEMPORARY GATHERING WORDS (1 JOHN 3)

Do you know who you are?
We are God's children.
That is who we are.
But who will you become?
We will become like Jesus
when we see him as he is.
What then should we do?
We will purify ourselves
as Christ is pure.
Come; let us worship God.

CONTEMPORARY GATHERING WORDS (LUKE 24, EASTER)

See the wounds on his hands and feet.
Christ is risen!
Hear the words of scripture revealed.
Christ is risen!
Christ is risen!
Christ is risen indeed!

PRAISE SENTENCES (ACTS 3, LUKE 24)

The sick are healed!
Christ is risen!

The dead are raised!
Christ is risen!
Christ is risen!
Christ is risen indeed!

OPENING PRAYER (LUKE 24, JOHN 21)
Tender-loving God,
    you come to us in our weakness
        and do not put us to shame.
When Jesus appeared to his disciples,
    he gently showed them the wounds
        on his hands and feet.
When Jesus confronted the disciples' lack of faith,
    he shared a meal of broiled fish with them,
    and opened their minds
        to the meaning of the scriptures.
Come to us in our moments of doubt and loss,
    and lead us back into the knowledge
        of your everlasting love,
    that we might proclaim your salvation
        for all to hear. Amen.

OPENING PRAYER (1 JOHN 3)
Merciful God,
    you come to us in our confusion and self-doubt
        to teach us who we are and whose we are.
You have made us your children,
    put your own image within us,
    and promised to make us like your Son
        revealed in the fullness of your glory.
Help us to purify ourselves, as Christ is pure,
    that we may be a righteous people,
    free from lawlessness and sin.
Teach us to abide in Christ Jesus,
    that the powers of darkness
        may have no hold over us.

In the name of the One who was
and is and is to come. Amen.

BENEDICTION (ACTS 3)
May the God of Abraham and Sarah
bless you and keep you.
We go with God's blessings.
May the God of Isaac and Rebecca
shine upon your life.
We go with God's blessings.
May the God of Jacob and Rachel
be gracious unto you.
We go with God's blessings.
May the God of Jesus Christ
grant you peace.

BENEDICTION (LUKE 24)
Go as witnesses of the Risen Lord.
Christ has fed us and made us whole.
Go as witnesses of the Risen Lord.
Christ has revealed God's word to us.
Go as witnesses of the Risen Lord.
Christ has raised us to newness of life.

MAY 7, 2006

Fourth Sunday of Easter
Mary Scifres

COLOR
White

SCRIPTURE READINGS
Acts 4:5-12; Psalm 23; 1 John 3:16-24; John 10:11-18

THEME IDEAS
The Good Shepherd and the mighty shepherding love of Christ are the focus of today's readings. Even as Acts focuses on the unique saving ability of Jesus Christ, John implies that other sheep will become a part of God's fold through the shepherding guidance of Jesus. The familiar words of Psalm 23 become fresh when intertwined with the words of John 10 and the love-in-action of 1 John 3.

CALL TO WORSHIP (PSALM 23)
Lead us into worship.
May we sense your mercy in this time and place.
Lead us into praise.
Help us to see goodness all around.
Lead us in your peace.
Let us walk beside your waters of life.
Lead us in the sacrament of grace.
Let us rejoice in the cup that overflows.
Lead us into worship.
Let us walk in the light of your love.

CALL TO WORSHIP (JOHN 10, 1 JOHN 3)

The Good Shepherd is calling.
We come, abiding in love.
The Shepherd of Love is calling.
We come, living in faith.
The Shepherd of Life is calling.
We hear, trusting in God's word.

CONTEMPORARY GATHERING WORDS (ACTS 4, JOHN 10)

Jesus is our firm foundation.
Praise Christ, our cornerstone!
Jesus is our loving shepherd.
Praise Christ, our cornerstone!
Jesus is our gracious savior.
Praise Christ, our cornerstone!

PRAISE SENTENCES (PSALM 23)

The Lord is our shepherd, giving all that we need.
Praise God, who cares so much!
The Lord is our shepherd, giving all that we need.
Praise God who cares so much.

OPENING PRAYER (PSALM 23)

Shepherding God,
    lead us into this time of worship.
Help us to rest in your presence,
    and trust in your grace.
Prepare our hearts,
    just as you have prepared this time for us.
And grant us the goodness and mercy that are ours,
    when we abide in your love,
    and dwell in your grace,
    all the days of our lives. Amen.

OPENING PRAYER (1 JOHN 3)

Thank you, Lover of our souls,
> for giving us the gift of worship.

Thank you for bringing us into your presence,
> and for showering us with your love.

As we worship and praise,
> touch our hearts and minds,
> > that we may prepare to live in your love
> > > and abide in your grace,
> > > today and all days. Amen.

PRAYER OF COMMITMENT OR OFFERING PRAYER (1 JOHN 3)

God of love and grace,
> we know that you have called us
> > to abide in your love.

We know that you trust us
> to live that love
> > in word and deed.

Accept our gifts and our lives,
> that we might be your servants of love.

Transform these offerings and our ministries,
> that we might be instruments of your grace.

Abide in us, dear Lord,
> that your love might shine through us
> > and into all the world. Amen.

BENEDICTION (1 JOHN 3)

Abide in love,
for by this we are known.
> **We leave in God's care,**
> **taking love wherever we go.**

Abide in love,
for by this we are named.
> **We leave in God's name,**
> **taking Christ where we go.**

Abide in love,
for by this we are saved.
**We leave in God's grace,
sharing mercy with all.**

BENEDICTION (PSALM 23)

Now may God our Shepherd lead us forth.
May the one who gives us everything we need
    lead us on steady paths and righteous roads.
And may the goodness and mercy of our Lord Jesus Christ
    guide us and follow us on all the journeys we face.

MAY 14, 2006

Fifth Sunday of Easter
Festival of the Christian Home
Mother's Day
Laura Jaquith Bartlett

COLOR
White

SCRIPTURE READINGS
Acts 8:26-40; Psalm 22:25-31; 1 John 4:7-21; John 15:1-8

THEME READINGS
Love! We take it for granted. We use it as a casual sign-off to instant messages. We commercialize it on Valentine's Day, and yes, even on Mother's Day. Today's scriptures call us back to the real power of love in Jesus Christ. Both the epistle and the gospel readings speak, albeit in somewhat esoteric terms, of the pull that God's love has in our lives. When we truly love, it is reflected in our relationships with others (including the relationship between mothers and children) and it can be seen in the fruit we bear. But the Acts story is the grand climax. Here we see a concrete illustration of the amazing transformative power of God's love. And the good news is that God's love is still available to change our lives today!

CALL TO WORSHIP (1 JOHN 4)

Jesus invites us, saying: "Abide in me as I abide in you."
We live in Jesus Christ!
"Those who abide in me bear much fruit."
We live in Jesus Christ!
"If you abide in me, you become my disciples."
We live in Jesus Christ! Alleluia!

CALL TO WORSHIP (PSALM 22)

Our praise comes from God.
Let the whole congregation praise the Lord.
God fills the hungry.
Let all those who seek God praise the Lord.
All the ends of the earth shall remember
and turn to the Lord.
Let the families of all the nations worship God.
Praise the Lord!

CONTEMPORARY GATHERING WORDS (1 JOHN 4)

Beloved friends, we gather together in love.
Our love for one another reflects the true love
of God.
God's love has been shown to us through the gift
of the Son.
Our love for one another embodies
the compassionate love of Jesus.
We come together unafraid, for we know that perfect
love casts out fear.
Our love for one another is empowered
by the fearless movement of the Spirit.

PRAISE SENTENCES (1 JOHN 4)

We love because God first loved us.
Perfect love casts out fear!
If we love one another, God lives in us.
God is love!

PRAISE SENTENCES (1 JOHN 4)

Beloved, let us love one another.
Love is from God.
Everyone who loves is born of God.
Everyone who loves knows God.
God is love!

OPENING PRAYER (1 JOHN 4)

Loving God,
  you drench us with your love each day.
When we make you our home,
  your love showers out of us
    in every relationship,
    every word, every action.
Help us to use your love as our badge of courage,
  casting out our fears,
  going forth each day to proclaim your good news,
  and showing your love to this world
    that so desperately needs it.
We pray in the name of the One
  through whom your love was revealed,
  Jesus Christ. Amen.

OPENING PRAYER (1 JOHN 4, JOHN 15)

Dear God,
Your love is life-changing,
  but there are times we don't want to change.
Your love is begging to be proclaimed
  throughout the world,
  but it's easier to just keep quiet.
Your love challenges us to love *all* our sisters
  and brothers around the globe,
  but it just seems too difficult.
Your love invites us to live in you completely,
  but it's so easy to turn our backs on you.
Great God of Love,

open our hearts, guide our actions,
restore and renew us.
Prune away the unproductive wood
and lead us back into new growth
in the sunshine of your love. Amen.

WORDS OF ASSURANCE (1 JOHN 4)
When we know God, we know love.
God lives in each of us.
And so God's love lives in each of us.
Grow in the warmth of God's love!

PRAYER OF CONFESSION (JOHN 15)
God the vine-grower,
we do not always want to be pruned.
We become attached to our branches,
and we're afraid of the pain
that comes with letting go.
Help us to trust your care, O God,
and open our eyes to see the vision of new growth
and full harvest which you promise.
We pray that we might give ourselves completely to you,
losing our fear and trusting your love.
Guide us as we seek to train our branches
to grow in harmony with the true vine,
your Son Jesus. Amen.

WORDS OF ASSURANCE
Jesus tells us that we have already been cleansed
by the word that he has spoken to us.
God's love makes us new each day.

BENEDICTION (1 JOHN 4, JOHN 15)
Beloved friends, go in God's love, live in Christ's love,
and be nurtured by the Spirit's love.
Grow in love and bear the fruit of the Vine. Amen.

BENEDICTION (1 JOHN 4)
Love one another, as God loves you.
We go to show God's love in the world.
Love one another, as Christ loves you.
We go to be Christ's disciples in the world.
Love one another, as the Spirit loves you.
We go to live in unity in the world.

MAY 21, 2006

Sixth Sunday of Easter
Sara Dunning Lambert

COLOR
White

SCRIPTURE READINGS
Acts 10:44-48; Psalm 98; 1 John 5:1-6; John 15:9-17

THEME IDEAS
In Acts, we see the Holy Spirit poured out "even on the Gentiles," evidence that the good news is meant for all. The psalm is filled with praise for a victorious God as ruler and judge. The epistle is concerned with faith that conquers the world for Christ. John reiterates the new commandment to love one another as Christ loves us. These verses come together to guide us toward an outward looking faith that must be shared, spreading the love that comes from the best and highest love we know—the sacrifice made by the Son of God.

CALL TO WORSHIP (PSALM 98, ACTS 10)
We come with open hearts to worship the Risen Christ!
Sing praises to the Lord!
Make a joyful noise before the king.
Sing a new song. God has done marvelous things!
May the gift of the Holy Spirit pour out on us today.
In faith and hope, we seek God's love. Amen!

CALL TO WORSHIP (JOHN 15)

God loves us, and so we must love one another.
We abide in God's love together.
The new commandment insists that we love one another
as Christ loved us.
We abide in Christ's love together.
The promise of the Holy Spirit is love without end.
We abide in the Spirit's love together.
Jesus said these things so that our joy might be complete.
Amen!

CALL TO WORSHIP (ACTS 10, PSALM 98)

In the spirit of truth,
    we come together seeking Christ's victory
        in our hearts and in our lives.
Let us greet God's word with joyful openness.
And as we begin to discern the Holy Spirit
    pouring God's blessing into our minds and prayers,
    let us be grateful.
As we worship, may the Lord's steadfast love
    be apparent in all we do and say. Amen.

CONTEMPORARY GATHERING WORDS (1 JOHN 5)

Everyone who believes in Jesus has been born of God.
Hallelujah, Christ is risen!
Our faith assures the victory of Christ in the world.
Hallelujah, Christ is risen!
The Holy Spirit guides us to the truth.
Hallelujah, Christ is risen!
Let us rejoice!
Hallelujah, Christ is risen!
Christ is risen indeed!

PRAISE SENTENCES (PSALM 98, 1 JOHN 5)

Make a joyful noise to the Lord for God is great!
"Sing to the Lord a new song

for God has done marvelous things!"
May the Holy Spirit pour out on us today!
Because Christ loved us, we must love one another.
Spread the good news to all the world. Jesus loves you!

OPENING PRAYER (1 JOHN 5, JOHN 15)

Lord, as your beloved children,
we need your guidance and your concern.
We seek to obey your commandment
to love one another, that by our example
the world may know the depth of your love.
Show us the way to your truth,
through Jesus Christ our Lord. Amen.

UNISON PRAYER OR PRAYER OF CONFESSION

Loving God,
you envelop us in a parent's warm embrace,
teaching us to love others,
and molding us to grow in faith.
In your wisdom, we ask for strength in obedience,
as we sometimes stray from your commandments.
As a child asks its mother for forgiveness,
we ask once again, with broken hearts,
for your patience with our infirmities.
Guide us in the way of truth,
that we might always follow you. Amen.

WORDS OF ASSURANCE (1 JOHN 5)

Hear these words of assurance:
"Everyone who believes that Jesus is the Christ
has been born of God."
Our Parent God claims us as children of God.
Know that God's love has no bounds.
All who come are taken into the warmth
of God's forgiveness. Amen.

BENEDICTION (1 JOHN 5, 1 JOHN 15)

All you who believe, love each other as Christ loved you.
For faith and love, born of God's grace,
    will conquer the world.
Go out with courage, abiding in love now and forever.
Amen.

BENEDICTION (ACTS 10, PSALM 98)

The world awaits!
Feel the Holy Spirit at work in you,
    shouting a new song of God's steadfast love!
Make joyful noises as you disperse
    to share the Good News of the Risen Christ!
Hallelujah!

MAY 28, 2006

Seventh Sunday of Easter
Ascension Sunday

Jack P. Miller

COLOR
White

ASCENSION SUNDAY READINGS
Acts 1:1-11; Psalm 47; Ephesians 1:15-23; Luke 24:44-53

SEVENTH SUNDAY AFTER EASTER READINGS
Acts 1:15-17, 21-26; Psalm 1; 1 John 5:9-13; John 17:6-19

THEME IDEAS
Jesus the Christ has ascended beyond our realm of experience, extending salvation to all time and space. Often, we are found peering upward, as if we could limit him to our spheres of comprehension. Messengers from heaven could scarcely draw us toward the larger picture we need to see.

CALL TO WORSHIP (ACTS 1)
On your feet! Rise up! Be on high alert!
This Jesus has gone, but is not missing.
I tell you a mystery:
    when you least expect, he is there.
This is why we gather as believers:

to watch and pray together,
lest we miss the moment of his appearing.

CALL TO WORSHIP (ACTS 1)

Come together, Christians!
How long will you stand gawking at empty clouds?
Our Lord has promised to go and prepare a place for us,
and to come again on our behalf.
We need not die to claim this promise!
Look around you for signs of his presence,
even in this hour of worship.

CALL TO WORSHIP (ACTS 1, LUKE 24)

Come, Lord Jesus.
Come, Lord Jesus, once again.
Do not leave us here alone.
Do not leave us comfortless.
We wait for the coming of the Holy Spirit.
We wait. We hope.
We lift our heads and hearts.
We worship and wait.
We worship and wait.

GATHERING WORDS (ROMANS 8, EPHESIANS 1, LUKE 24)

Nothing! Neither death ... life ... angels ... empires ...
things present or things to come ... powers ...
height ... depth ... nor anything else in all creation
can separate us from the love of God in Christ Jesus
our Lord.
When Jesus disappeared from his disciples' sight,
their hearts burned within them all the more.
He ascended, he descended; it matters not at all;
for Christ is in all, around all, above all, and all in all,
now and forevermore.

CONTEMPORARY GATHERING WORDS (ACTS 2)
Is your burden heavy?
Does your heart hurt?
Do you long for a comforter?
Come, and be marinated in the Spirit!

PRAISE SENTENCES (LUKE 24)
Jesus is the Lord of all creation.
Anywhere I may be, he is there too.
I will stay in the city, just like he said.
I will wait until the power of the Lord comes down.

OPENING PRAYER (EASTER, ASCENSION, LUKE 24, ACTS 1)
God of grace and surprise,
    keep us watching for signs of the Risen Christ.
Remind us that we tread on holy ground,
    a world shot through with divine presence
    and possibility.
We set aside this hour
    gazing at the skies on tiptoe,
    watching with gladness for Christ
    who fills all things. Amen.

PRAYER OF CONFESSION (ACTS 1)
Dear God,
    grant that our time of worship may inspire us
    to leave this place as peacemakers and joygivers.
For the times when our gaze was so fixed upward
    that we failed to live outward toward your children,
    forgive us.
For having our heads in the clouds
    when Jesus is by our side,
        dear Lord save us!
Even as we persist in our foolish ways,
    keep us as your own.

May we partake of your mercy as freely as you give,
through Jesus Christ our Lord. Amen.

WORDS OF ASSURANCE (FROM ROMANS 8:3 IN THE MESSAGE)

"The Spirit of life in Christ, like a strong wind,
has magnificently cleared the air, freeing you from sin
and death." In Jesus Christ, you are forgiven!
In Jesus Christ, you are forgiven!

BENEDICTION

Live each day as carefully as if you had no more:
with no sin unrepented,
no apology postponed,
and no one unblessed as you pass by.
Go in the grace of Jesus Christ!

BENEDICTION

Go and serve the Lord in strong and honest ways,
that you might be for others a sign of Jesus Christ.
As you journey on,
may your wanderings weave God's design,
and may your love leave many trails.

BENEDICTION

Find the path God puts before you,
and let your steps be strong.
Walk humbly, but love extravagantly,
that when you are called to give account of your life,
you may come into God's presence with gladness.

JUNE 4, 2006

Pentecost Sunday
Robert Blezard

COLOR
Red

SCRIPTURE READINGS
Acts 2:1-21; Psalm 104:24-34, 35*b*; Romans 8:22-27; John 15:26-27; 16:4*b*-15

THEME IDEAS
There was no ignoring the Holy Spirit on the day of Pentecost. In rushing wind and tongues of flame, the Spirit made a dramatic entrance to the crowd of Christians gathered from near and far. Quite a contrast to the second person of the trinity who was born in a humble stable and spent most of his earthly ministry deflecting attention away from himself. Today we celebrate the Holy Spirit among us—as an advocate, comforter, helper, and encourager in our lives and in our ministries. We remember today that the Spirit's first act was to dissolve language barriers among Christians of many nations, so that they could understand one another. In today's world, where Christians are separated not only by language but also by politics and ideology, we need the Spirit's gift of mutual understanding.

CALL TO WORSHIP (ACTS 2)
In rushing wind. In tongues of flame.
Come, Holy Spirit !

Fill our house of worship.
Come, Holy Spirit!
Open our ears to hear one another.
Come Holy Spirit!
Gather your people from everywhere.
Come, Holy Spirit!
Teach us to understand one another.
Come, Holy Spirit!

CALL TO WORSHIP (ACTS 2)

On Pentecost day, people came from all over.
Unite us, Holy Spirit!
They came from Rome, Crete, Egypt, and Galilee.
Unite us, Holy Spirit!
They all spoke in their native tongues.
Unite us, Holy Spirit!
Through the Spirit, they all understood as one.
Unite us, Holy Spirit.
Today, many issues divide your people.
Unite us, Holy Spirit!
Politics, class, culture, prejudice and pride.
Unite us, Holy Spirit!
In our weaknesses help us to stand.
Unite us, Holy Spirit!
Make us one people, young and old, woman and man.
Unite us, Holy Spirit!

CALL TO WORSHIP (ROMANS 8)

We groan inwardly as we wait for God.
We do not know how to pray as we ought.
We place our hope in what is yet unseen.
We do not know how to pray as we ought.
But God's Spirit helps us in our weaknesses.
And intercedes with sighs too deep for words.

CONTEMPORARY GATHERING WORDS (ACTS 2, JOHN 15, JOHN 16)

God's Spirit is with us!
We are one in God's Love.
God's Spirit renews us!
We are alive in God's Love.
God's Spirit teaches us!
We have hope in God's love.

PRAISE SENTENCES (PSALM 104)

How great is the work of our Lord!
God made creatures, both great and small.
The Lord has filled us with good things.
God's Spirit nourishes us all.

PRAISE SENTENCES (PSALM 104, ACTS 2)

Let us bring praises to our God,
    through our meditations, our songs and our mirth.
Rejoice in God's Holy Spirit,
    the Spirit that renews the face of the earth.

OPENING PRAYER (ACTS 2)

Almighty and everlasting God,
    your Holy Spirit came to the saints in Jerusalem
        in the rushing of violent wind and tongues of flames,
        that filled the whole house.
We welcome the breath and flame of your Spirit today
    in this house of worship.
Renew us with your love and life. Amen.

OPENING PRAYER (ROMANS 8)

Give us your Holy Spirit, O God,
    for we have been groaning
        and waiting for our adoption and redemption.
Our hope is in you, O God.
You help us in our weaknesses.

Let your Spirit intercede for us,
according to your will. Amen.

UNISON (ACTS 2, PSALM 104, ROMANS 8)

O God, by your Holy Spirit,
you gather, unite, and stir your people to action.
We long to stand together as your children,
called to your purposes.
You nourish your children
and fill them with good things.
We lift our voices and songs to you,
in whom we have our hope.
You pour your Spirit over all of creation,
changing and renewing our lives.
We patiently await the coming of your Spirit,
when our sons and our daughters shall prophesy,
and our young and old shall see visions.
We want to live prophetic lives.
We want to have purpose and vision.

RESPONSIVE READING (ROMANS 8:22-27)

We know that the whole creation
has been groaning in labor pains until now.
And not only the creation, but we ourselves,
who have the firstfruits of the Spirit,
groan inwardly while we wait for adoption,
the redemption of our bodies.
For in hope we were saved.
Now hope that is seen is not hope.
For who hopes for what is seen?
But if we hope for what we do not see,
we wait for it with patience.
Likewise the Spirit helps us in our weakness.
For we do not know how to pray as we ought,
but that very Spirit intercedes
with sighs too deep for words.

And God, who searches the heart,
knows what is the mind of the Spirit,
because the Spirit intercedes for the saints
according to the will of God.

BENEDICTION (ROMANS 8)

May God's Spirit renew us, strengthen us,
    guide us, nourish us and intercede for us.
As redeemed children of God,
    let us go forth with confidence to love God
    and serve our neighbor.

BENEDICTION (JOHN 15, JOHN 16)

You are created by God; redeemed by God's Son;
    and sustained by God's Holy Spirit.
Now go in God's peace.

JUNE 11, 2006

Trinity Sunday
B. J. Beu

COLOR
White

SCRIPTURE READINGS
Isaiah 6:1-8; Psalm 29; Romans 8:12-17; John 3:1-17

THEME IDEAS
Trinity Sunday is a time to celebrate the fullness of God in the persons of the Father, Son, and Holy Spirit. Christians understand that the God Isaiah experiences face-to-face in the Temple is the same God that Paul proclaims as the Father of Jesus Christ—the One who adopts us as children of God through the power of the Holy Spirit. This triune God is the One revealed by Christ when he was lifted up to bring us eternal life. The inner life of God is so holy, so awesome, that when we are brought into communion with God, we are truly born from above.

CALL TO WORSHIP (PSALM 29)
Worship the Lord in holy splendor.
Who is like our God in glory and strength?
The voice of the Lord thunders over the mighty waters.
The voice of God breaks the cedars.
The voice of the Lord flashes forth like flames of fire.

The voice of God shakes the wilderness.
The Lord sits enthroned over the flood.
God sits enthroned as king forever.
Come; let us worship the Lord!

CALL TO WORSHIP (JOHN 3)
Come; let us be born of water and the Spirit.
We have come to be born anew.
Come; let us worship the One
who brings us everlasting life.
We have come to be born anew.
Come; let us worship God.

CONTEMPORARY GATHERING WORDS (ROMANS 8)
Why are we here?
The Spirit has led us here
to become God's children.
Rejoice, children of God,
for God has made us heirs with Christ.
In Christ, we are adopted into God's family
and glorified with him.
Freed from fear, let us worship God together.
Amen.

PRAISE SENTENCES (ROMANS 8)
The Spirit gives us life.
We are God's children.
The Spirit frees us from fear.
We are brothers and sisters of Christ.
The Spirit gives us life.

PRAISE SENTENCES (JOHN 3)
We are born of the Spirit.
God has saved us.
We are born of the Spirit.
Christ has saved us.

We are born of the Spirit.
We are born anew in God.

OPENING PRAYER (ROMANS 8, JOHN 3)
O God,
   your Spirit calls us here.
Help us to be born anew,
   not in the flesh,
   but with water and the Spirit.
In Christ, you have adopted us into your family
   and made us heirs to your kingdom.
We are your precious children,
   and you are our God.
We thank you.
May our lives proclaim in everything we do
   that your Son came not to condemn the world
      but to save it. Amen.

OPENING PRAYER OR PRAYER OF CONFESSION (ISAIAH 6)
God of power and might,
   seraphs and angels proclaim your glory
      throughout the earth.
We shrink before the majesty of your throne,
   for your holiness is more than we can bear.
We feel lost in your presence,
   for we are an unclean people
      with unclean lips.
Touch our mouths
   that we might be made clean.
Send us forth as your people,
   that we may go where you send us.
Help us say with your prophet Isaiah,
   "Here I am, send me." Amen.

ASSURANCE OF PARDON (ROMANS 8)

God has not given us a spirit of slavery to fear,
but a spirit of strength and truth.
When we are led by the Holy Spirit,
we are God's children
and receive a spirit of adoption.
In Christ, we share in God's glory and victory.
Through the power of the Spirit,
our sins are forgiven. Amen.

BENEDICTION (ISAIAH 6)

The Lord of hosts awaits.
Who will go to serve our God?
We want to go, but are afraid.
How can we stand before God's holiness?
The Lord of hosts awaits.
Who will go to serve our God?
We want to go, but feel unworthy.
We are an unclean people with unclean lips.
The Lord of hosts awaits.
Who will go to serve our God?
Cleanse us, O God, and we will be made whole.
We are your servants Lord. Send us.

BENEDICTION (JOHN 3)

Christ has come to save us.
We are born anew.
The Spirit has come to save us.
We are born again.
Go with the blessings of Christ, who came,
not to condemn the world, but to save it.
We go with the blessings of Almighty God.

JUNE 18, 2006

Second Sunday after Pentecost
Father's Day

Erik Alsgaard

COLOR

Green

SCRIPTURE READINGS

1 Samuel 15:34–16:13; Psalm 20; 2 Corinthians 5:6-10
(11-13), 14-17; Mark 4:26-34

THEME IDEAS

An old cliché is the familiar, "never judge a book by its
cover." Today's lectionary readings provide ample evidence of that. God does not look on the outside of a person, but rather on the inside: the character, heart, soul,
and spirit of a person. Nor does God use only the
"biggest and the best." Both David's selection as the next
king of Israel and the parable of the mustard seed—
paired here today—point out that God will use whom
God will use to fulfill God's purposes. And as we celebrate Father's Day today, we acknowledge that even
with all the human imperfections fathers possess, where
there is love of God, there is love to be shared and grown.

CALL TO WORSHIP (MARK 4)

A tiny seed planted in the ground grows to a mighty bush.
God's kingdom is like this.

A bush puts forth large branches.
God's kingdom is like this.
A bush provides shelter and shade to one and to all.
God's kingdom is like this.
We worship the One who makes all things possible.
God's kingdom is like that!

CALL TO WORSHIP (2 CORINTHIANS 5)

The love of Christ urges us on.
**We are convinced that Christ has died for us
and for our salvation.**
Jesus died that we may live,
and share in life everlasting.
God teaches us to regard no one
from a human point of view.
**God sees the strength of our character,
our heart and our spirit.**
When we are in Christ Jesus, we are a new creation.
**Everything old has passed away.
Thanks be to God!**

CALL TO WORSHIP (PSALM 20)

I called out to the Lord in my time of trouble.
The Lord has answered me!
I sought the joys of my heart's desire.
The Lord has answered me!
I will shout with joy because of the victories
God has worked in my life.
The Lord has answered me!
Our pride is in the name of the Lord our God,
our victorious King.
The Lord has answered me!

CONTEMPORARY GATHERING WORDS (MARK 4)

Though our faith may be as tiny as the smallest seed,
God can do miracles with what we offer.

Though our offerings may be planted among the weeds,
God creates victories where we least expect them.
God has planted in each of us the seeds of faith,
God can do great things, especially in me.
Create in me a clean heart, O God,
that what you give may be multiplied.
God will do miracles in our lives!

PRAISE SENTENCES (PSALM 20)

The Lord answers us in our times of trouble.
We shout for joy in God's victories in our lives.
Some take pride in things of this world,
but our pride is in the name of the Lord our God.

OPENING PRAYER (MARK 4)

Almighty God,
you are able to take the least, the last, and the lost,
and use them to your glory.
Enable us to see with the eyes of your heart,
to listen with the ears of your love,
and to live with the strength of your spirit,
that in all we do as the Body of Christ,
your name would be glorified
and your kingdom created on earth.
In Jesus' name we pray. Amen.

OPENING PRAYER (1 SAMUEL 15)

O God,
help us remember that it is not in the might of height
or the strength of muscle that you choose us.
Increase in us the knowledge of your ways,
that we may be willing to give of ourselves freely,
not counting the cost but anticipating the gain.
May our lives be ones of constant searching
for the ways in which you are present,
and for ways in which we can bring your love

to a hurting world.
In Jesus' name we pray. Amen.

PRAYER OF CONFESSION (MARK 4)

Loving God,
when we think we know better than you—
when we know a tiny mustard seed
can't possibly help us,
when we shield a person from your grace and love,
convinced that you could never make use of them,
forgive us, we pray.
We have been taught never to judge a book by its cover,
and yet we cover your wisdom with our ignorance,
your grace with our stubbornness,
your new ways with our old ways.
Teach us, O God, to look for you
in unexpected and unusual places,
that we might break out of old molds
into new life.
In Jesus' precious name we pray. Amen.

BENEDICTION (PSALM 20)

This is a day of new beginnings.
This is our day of victory.
The Lord has taken us from our time of trouble,
and given us new life in the midst of trial.
Some say bigger is better, age equals wisdom,
and the race is won only by the swift.
But God says, I will give the victory
to those who call on my name.
O God, we shout for joy over the victories
you work in our lives.
This is our day of victory!

JUNE 25, 2006

Third Sunday after Pentecost
Mary Petrina Boyd

COLOR
Green

SCRIPTURE READINGS
1 Samuel 17:(1a, 4-11, 19-23) 32-49; Psalm 9:9-20;
2 Corinthians 6:1-13; Mark 4:35-41

THEME IDEAS
These scriptures express God's power to fight against
evil and to protect the oppressed and defenseless. While
the military imagery may be troubling to those of us who
live in abundance, the concept of a God who will save,
even when we feel powerless, speaks profoundly to
those who are oppressed. God pours out grace upon
David, the poor, the needy, the oppressed, and the frightened. The presence of God in our lives gives us courage
and destroys our fears.

CALL TO WORSHIP (PSALM 9)
The Lord is a stronghold in times of trouble.
We know God's name and trust in our Lord.
We trust in God, who will not forsake us.
God cares for the afflicted and the oppressed.
Sing praises to our God!
Tell God's great deeds to all people.

Rise up, O God. Hear our voices.
Rise up, O God. Save the oppressed.
Be gracious to us, O Lord.

CALL TO WORSHIP (1 SAMUEL 17, PSALM 9)

God calls us to be shepherds.
We will tenderly care for God's people.
God calls us to be warriors.
We will defend the powerless from evil.
God calls us to be heralds of God's mighty deeds.
We will sing praises and rejoice in Almighty God.

CALL TO WORSHIP (MARK 9)

When the waves of trouble overwhelm us,
you speak a word of peace.
When troubles gather around us,
you show us the way to safety.
When we doubt your power,
you lead us back to faith.

CONTEMPORARY GATHERING WORDS (1 SAMUEL 17)

Come be a shepherd.
We will care for the poor and the weak.
Come be a warrior.
We will defend the frightened from evil.
Come be God's people.
We will trust in God always.

CONTEMPORARY GATHERING WORDS (2 CORINTHIANS 6)

Now is the time to rejoice.
Now is the time for praise.
During great trials,
you give your people courage.

During sleepless nights,
you give your people peace
During every kind of trouble,
you sustain your people with love.
Now is the time to rejoice.
Now is the time for praise.

PRAISE SENTENCES (PSALM 9, MARK 4, 2 CORINTHIANS 6)

The Lord is our stronghold.
God will protect us!
God will defend us!
God is our hope.
Jesus calms the storm.
Jesus gives us peace!
Now is the acceptable time.
This is the day of salvation!

OPENING PRAYER (MARK 4)

God of wind and sea,
we come from the storm and tumult of life
to this quiet place of peace.
Let your love surround us,
bringing peace to our hearts.
In this time of worship,
silence our fears and strengthen our faith,
that we may live as your children. Amen.

UNISON PRAYER (1 SAMUEL 17, PSALM 9)

In a world of violence and tumult,
we turn to you O God.
You are our strength and our protector,
the source of comfort and peace.
We pray for those who are oppressed.
Defend them with your love,
and bring them comfort in times of trial.
We pray for the poor and needy,

whose daily struggles overwhelm them.
Stir up within us a passion for justice
  that we might serve you
    as we work for righteousness.
When warfare threatens the powerless,
  defend them by your might,
  and bring your peace
    to all the nations. Amen.

PRAYER OF CONFESSION (MARK 4)
God of power and might,
  we are so often afraid.
You call us to greatness,
  and we protest that we are weak.
You show us your ways,
  and we complain that they are too hard.
You promise to protect us,
  and we do not trust your word.
Forgive our weakness,
  and our lack of faith.
Strengthen us for your work,
  and your ministry in the world. Amen.

WORDS OF ASSURANCE
God speaks and the storm is still.
God speaks a word of peace.

BENEDICTION (1 SAMUEL 17, MARK 4)
As Jesus calmed the storm,
  Jesus brings us peace today.
Go forth in faith, with hearts of courage,
  to share God's peace with the world.

BENEDICTION (1 SAMUEL 17, MARK 4)
The Lord gives strength to the powerless,
  courage to the fearful,

faith to the doubting,
and peace to those who are afraid.
The Lord is our stronghold.
We are safe. Go in peace.

BENEDICTION (1 SAMUEL 17, MARK 4)
God transforms the weak and fearful.
God gives us power and might.
Declare God's deeds among the peoples.
Share God's peace with the world.

JULY 2, 2006

Fourth Sunday after Pentecost
Mary J. Scifres

COLOR
Green

SCRIPTURE READINGS
2 Samuel 1:1, 17-27; Psalm 130; 2 Corinthians 8:7-15; Mark 5:21-43

THEME IDEAS
Today's psalm and 2 Samuel readings offer poignant and powerful reflections on grief and loss, despair and sorrow. Used together, they present opportunities for services of lament and grief, or of repentance and petition for forgiveness. In 2 Corinthians, Paul challenges the church to give fully to its ministries and its calling, with particular emphasis on stewardship of material wealth. Mark's gospel weaves two incredibly moving stories of women who find health and wholeness through Jesus' miraculous power. The death of Jairus's daughter also offers possibilities for weaving the father's story of grief and hope with the words of grief and hope in today's readings from the Hebrew Scriptures.

CALL TO WORSHIP (MARK 5)
Come into the presence of Christ, who is our Healer.
Enter into the gates of hope.

Touch the garment of Jesus, who is our Life.
Encounter the hands that make us whole.
Come with your faith, your doubts, and your fears.
Christ welcomes all, and shows us the way.

CALL TO WORSHIP (PSALM 130)

Wait for the Lord, in whom we hope.
Worship the God of steadfast love.
Listen for Christ, who calls us here.
Open your hearts for the Spirit of God.

CALL TO WORSHIP (PSALM 130)

I wait for the Lord. My soul waits.
In the Lord's word I trust.
My soul waits for the Lord,
more than those who watch for the morning.
O Israel, hope in the Lord!
For with the Lord there is steadfast love.
With the Lord there is great power to redeem.
(Mary Petrina Boyd)

CONTEMPORARY GATHERING WORDS (PSALM 130, MARK 5)

In the depths of despair, we yearn for God.
In the darkness of night, we look for light.
In the sorrows of life, we long for hope.
Here in this place, Christ offers his touch.

CONTEMPORARY GATHERING WORDS (PSALM 130)

We are waiting.
We are waiting for God.
We are hoping.
We are hoping to hear God.
We are longing.

We are longing for God's presence.
God is here.
Let us rejoice! (Mary Petrina Boyd)

PRAISE SENTENCES (PSALM 130)

Wait for God, whose love is true!
Hope in the Lord, whose power is real.

PRAISE SENTENCES OR WORDS OF ASSURANCE (PSALM 130)

Even when we make mistakes, God is ready to forgive.
God's love is great and God is always faithful.
(Mary Petrina Boyd)

OPENING PRAYER (2 SAMUEL 1, PSALM 130, MARK 5)

O great Healer,
    send your power upon this place.
Touch our brokenness,
    and lift us up out of despair.
Walk with us on paths of fear,
    that we might discover faith and courage.
Dry the tears of our sorrow
    and show us the hope of new beginnings.
In your blessed name, we pray. Amen.

OPENING PRAYER (PSALM 130)

We wait for you, O God.
Waiting and hoping, we come.

OPENING PRAYER (MARK 5)

Christ Jesus,
    touch us in this hour.
Touch our lives and our souls.
Move our ministries and our moods.

Strengthen our faith and our hope.
Help us to live as people
    whose faith has indeed made us well.
Amen.

PRAYER OF LAMENT (2 SAMUEL 1, MARK 5)

Your glory, God, is shrouded and hidden in our midst.
All around, we see signs of death and decay.
    (time of silence)
Your strength and might are betrayed!
Your words are forgotten and your teachings are ignored!
    (time of silence)
We cry out in pain, in sorrow and grief.
We cry out in anger, in fear and despair.
    (time of silence)
We long for unity and strength.
We yearn for Christ's love, that overcomes hate.
    (time of silence)
Even as we lament the tragedies of life,
your love redeems us and makes us whole.
    (time of silence)
Come swiftly, Christ Jesus!
Redeem us and make us whole!

PRAYER (2 CORINTHIANS 8)

God of justice and generosity,
    help us to excel in faith and wisdom,
    in words and action.
Guide us as your stewards,
    that we may eagerly share
    the many gifts you have given us.
Help us to recognize
    the abundance of our lives,
    that we may share that abundance
    freely and lovingly.
With gratitude, we pray. Amen.

PRAYER OF CONFESSION (PSALM 130)

In our deep despair,
we call to you, O Yahweh!
Hear our prayers,
as we remember the many faults
and frailties of our lives.
Forgive us and redeem us,
that we may know your steadfast love
in all of its fullness. Amen.

WORDS OF ASSURANCE (PSALM 130)

Hope in the Lord, the one who made heaven and earth,
for God has heard our cries and answered our prayers.
We are redeemed by God's gracious love.
Amen and amen.

BENEDICTION (MARK 5)

Go forth with joy.
Your faith has made you well!

BENEDICTION (2 CORINTHIANS 8, MARK 5)

Remembering that Christ has begun a good work in you.
Go forth with faith and be made whole!

JULY 9, 2006

Fifth Sunday after Pentecost
Christine S. Boardman

COLOR
Green

SCRIPTURE READINGS
2 Samuel 5:1-5, 9-10; Psalm 48; 2 Corinthians 12:2-10;
Mark 6:1-13

THEME IDEAS
Today's scriptures highlight power and authority. As followers of Jesus and as leaders of the church, let us remember our definition and understanding of power for our daily lives in this world. We call on leaders to lead. We call on saviors to save. We call on the church to commune. Let's read our texts. The elders called David to be a powerful king. The psalmist labeled the City of God the most powerful place, above all other places. Paul called his weakness, power. Jesus came to visit his hometown and preached to them. They were offended by his power. We can imagine him shaking his head in disbelief over their disbelief. Could it be that as disciples of Jesus, our belief in God's greatness, steadfast love, guidance and grace is all the power we need in our lives? What power calls you to follow where Jesus leads?

CALL TO WORSHIP (PSALM 48, 2 CORINTHIANS 12, MARK 6)

We gather this day to praise God,
and to claim our inheritance as people of covenant.
Great is God's goodness and steadfast love.
We listen this day to hear God's word,
and to speak truth about the nature of true power.
Great is God's goodness and steadfast love.
We look this day to see God's way for our lives,
and find our footing as disciples of Jesus.
Great is God's goodness and steadfast love.
We know this day that God's goodness, love and grace
are sufficient for our lives, until the end of our days.
Let us worship God this day and sing God's praises.

CONTEMPORARY GATHERING WORDS

We wake-up. We wander. We wonder.
People of God, let us hold fast to our belief
    in the gospel of love and peace.
No earthly authority can claim our allegiance.
No earthly power can compare
    to the awesome power of God's love and peace.
Amen and amen.

PRAISE SENTENCES (PSALM 48)

God is worthy to be praised.
God is gracious.
God is love.
God is glorious.
Let us praise this glorious God.
Let us be gracious and loving.
Let us glory in this time of worship.

OPENING PRAYER (PSALM 48, MARK 6)

Gracious and loving God,
    we know you are mysterious and mighty.

We know you are everywhere,
and are in all things.
We know you are comforting and accepting.
If we can scale the highest mountain,
or dive to the deepest depth of the sea,
you are with us.
Your presence is beyond our imagination,
yet we feel this holy presence
as we worship together as your people.
Thank you for always going the distance with us,
no matter how far we wander away from you.
May the power of your love
claim our allegiance as disciples of Jesus,
who is the teacher and shepherd of our lives.
In his name, we pray. Amen.

PRAYER OF CONFESSION (2 CORINTHIANS 12, MARK 6)

Let us breathe in the life that God alone makes possible,
and breathe out all that would separate us from others.
**O Power of love, laughter, grace, and hope, hear
your people as we speak our fears, hopes, and needs.**
(time of silence)
You alone know who we are and who we want to be.
(time of silence)
**Empower, enlighten, and engage our lives with your
power.**
(time of silence)
**For ourselves, this church, our country, and the
world, soothe our pain, heal our hurt, and bring us
your blessing.**
(time of silence)
**Guide and direct our way when temptation leads us
to deny your image within ourselves and within
others. Forgive us, when we choose to act boastfully
or divisively.**

(time of silence)
Give us the strength to love and forgive, especially when it seems impossible. As your beloved people, help us to be truthful with you, ourselves, and others. Take us where you want us to be, as people of both belief and disbelief.
(time of silence)

WORDS OF ASSURANCE (MARK 6)
The dust has been swept away. The walk is clear.
People of the covenant, your life in Christ awaits you.
God's grace is sufficient. Amen.

BENEDICTION
As we leave one another and this holy place,
    may we be surrounded by the love of God
    like a comforting embrace.
May we be protected by the gracious presence
    of your Holy Spirit like a warm breeze.
May we be enlightened by the mind of Christ
    to seek the shadow and the light.
Go with goodness and with grace
    as God's beloved people.
Go in peace. Amen.

JULY 16, 2006

Sixth Sunday after Pentecost
Bill Hoppe

COLOR
Green

SCRIPTURE READINGS
2 Samuel 6:1-5, 12b-19; Psalm 24; Ephesians 1:3-14; Mark 6:14-29

THEME IDEAS
It's easy to imagine David singing what we know as Psalm 24, as he danced for joy before the Lord, when the Ark of God was brought into Jerusalem (2 Samuel 6). David praised the Lord without restraint, yet his wife, Michal, "despised him in her heart": the king of Israel had made a royal fool of himself. But "we are fools for Christ's sake," according to the apostle Paul, and should never feel ashamed to put our unbridled joy in the Lord on display for all to see. Using words, Paul dances before God in his own free-spirited way, as he offers praise to the Lord for every spiritual blessing—for being chosen in Christ before the world began (Ephesians 1). And then there's the grisly tale of the death of John the Baptist, which at first glance might seem out of place with the other readings, until we remember his own uninhibited ministry and service to God—right up to the end.

CALL TO WORSHIP (PSALM 24, EPHESIANS 1)

The earth is the Lord's, and all that is in it.
In Christ, we were chosen before the world began.
The world is the Lord's, and we who live in it.
God calls us to be holy, blameless, and full of love.
Who shall stand before the Lord in this holy place?
All with clean hands and pure hearts—
all who speak the truth.
In Christ, we have redemption and forgiveness.
In Christ, we have become God's own people.

CONTEMPORARY GATHERING WORDS (PSALM 24)

Lift your heads! Lift yourselves up!
Open the gates! Open the doors!
Make way for the king of glory!
Make way for the Lord of hosts!

CONTEMPORARY GATHERING WORDS (2 SAMUEL 6)

Unafraid, unashamed ...
unbridled, unchained, unrestrained ...
uninhibited, unconcealed ...
we're unable to keep God's love to ourselves!

CONTEMPORARY GATHERING WORDS (2 SAMUEL 6, EPHESIANS 1, MARK 6)

David danced, John spoke, Paul wrote.
David sang, John baptized, Paul preached.
A king praised the Lord with all his might.
Prisoners stood firm in the truth.
How has God been revealed through you?

PRAISE SENTENCES (2 SAMUEL 6, PSALM 24, EPHESIANS 1)

We will dance for joy before the Lord!
All who seek God receive a blessing!
God's purpose is at work everywhere!

OPENING PRAYER (2 SAMUEL 6)

Our souls dance before you today, Lord,
  with unbridled joy—
  with unconcealed abandon.
We spin before you
  as clay spins on a potter's wheel,
  deliriously happy to become vessels
  fit for your service,
  ready to be filled with your spirit.
We shout your praise for all the world to hear.
We sing our thanks for your presence among us!
We love you and worship you.
And we're unafraid to show it,
  as we pray together in your wonderful name.
Amen!

OPENING PRAYER (EPHESIANS 1)

Praise be to you, Lord,
  for giving us every spiritual blessing under heaven;
  for making us all your children through Christ;
  for sharing with us your hidden purpose,
    that all in heaven and earth
      may be brought into unity through you.
You've redeemed us, sealed us,
  and shared the richness of your free grace with us.
You've secured our release,
  and you've secured our hearts forever.
Praise and glory be yours, Lord! Amen.

PRAYER OF CONFESSION

Lord, you've called us to be light for the world,
  yet we often find ourselves hiding this light,
  selfishly keeping it to ourselves.
You present us with many opportunities
  to do your will, and to share your word of truth
  with those who need it so desperately.

Why do we remain silent?
Why are we afraid to speak?
How can we, who have been transformed by your love,
    withhold its life-changing power from others?
Help us to hear your call of repentance,
    and turn our hearts back to you,
    as your servant John the Baptist implored all to do.
Give us fearless conviction like his,
    that with determination and courage
    we may tell your truth in love to the world,
    no matter the situation.
In the name of Christ, who set us free, amen.

WORDS OF ASSURANCE (EPHESIANS 1, PSALM 24)

In Christ, our release has been secured
    through the shedding of his blood.
Through Jesus, we've been given clean hands
    and pure hearts.
In him, we've received the Lord's blessing.
We've received vindication
    from the God of our salvation.
This is the inheritance of redemption
    for all who seek the Lord,
    and for all who seek the face of God.

BENEDICTION (EPHESIANS 2)

Praise be to the One
    whose will and pleasure is at work in you;
    who, through Jesus, claims you as children.
Praise be to the One
    whose purpose is revealed through you;
    who has lavished free grace upon you;
    who imparts true wisdom and insight.

Praise and glory to God,
    who brings all into unity in Christ! Amen.

JULY 23, 2006

Seventh Sunday after Pentecost
Bill Hoppe

COLOR
Green

SCRIPTURE READINGS
2 Samuel 7:1-14*a*; Psalm 89:20-37; Ephesians 2:11-22; Mark 6:30-34, 53-56

THEME IDEAS
From 2 Samuel 7 and Psalm 89, we learn of God's promise to King David that his house and lineage would be established forever. Through this promise, and God's actions and promises found in Mark's gospel and the letter to the Ephesians, we see that the Lord is at work everywhere in our need, no matter how near or faraway it may be. The household of God also thematically ties these scriptures together. No matter how near or how far away we may have been, the Lord has brought us all together underneath one roof. The community of Israel, including the house of David, has been made one with the Gentiles, reconciled in a single body. David wanted to build God a dwelling place on earth, but in Christ, this spiritual structure is already joined together. In Christ, we have become the holy temple of God.

CALL TO WORSHIP OR BENEDICTION (PSALM 89)

O God, you showed favor to your servant David.
Anoint us also with your holy oil, O Lord.
Your hands are always ready to help us
Your arms give us strength.
Your true love is ever with us.
In your name, we will hold our heads high!
You are our Lord; you are our God.
You are the Rock of our salvation!
Blessed is the Lord forever!
Blessed is the Lord! Amen.

CALL TO WORSHIP (EPHESIANS 2)

Peace to all who are far off; peace to all who are near!
Christ Jesus is our peace!
Peace to all, saints and citizens, strangers no longer!
Christ Jesus is our peace!
Peace to all, built together into the dwelling place of God!
Christ Jesus is our peace!

CONTEMPORARY GATHERING WORDS (2 SAMUEL 7, EPHESIANS 2)

Who are we to build a house for God?
Who are we to think such a thing?
God is always moving about.
When has the Lord asked us for a house?
Instead, God has broken down the walls that divide us.
In Christ, we're joined together into a new structure.
We have become the holy living temple of the Lord!

CONTEMPORARY GATHERING WORDS (MARK 6)

What was it like, Lord?
You and the disciples barely had a chance to eat—
you were all so busy.
What was it like, Lord?
Each time you tried to find a quiet place

to rest and to renew your strength,
you were recognized and followed.
People came from everywhere to see you,
to hear you, to feel your healing touch.
Lord, what was it like?
Wherever you went, people arrived there first,
no matter where you decided to go.
In the villages and towns, across the countryside,
the sick were laid out in the marketplaces,
waiting for you, begging to be made whole.
You never hesitated to reach out your hand
to those in need.
Your heart always went out to those who sought you.
O Lord, what was it like? What was it like?

PRAISE SENTENCES (PSALM 89)

God's love is faithful!
God's love is forever!
God's love is as faithful as the moon's appearance.
God's love is as eternal as the heavens above!

OPENING PRAYER (MARK 6)

Lead us, Lord. Wherever you go, we'll follow you there.
Wherever we are, we'll hurry to meet you.
Teach us, Lord. We're like sheep without a shepherd.
We need your instruction.
We need your compassion.
Heal us, Lord. Simply touch us, and we'll be cured.
Let us touch you, and we'll be made whole. Amen.

PRAYER OF CONFESSION (PSALM 89)

We can't help ourselves, Lord,
try as we may,
we always seem to forget your teachings;
we always seems to ignore your judgments.
We renounce your word,

and we fail to follow your commandments.
Our disobedience deserves your punishment,
    yet you have promised us your steadfast love.
Lord, your faithfulness has always proved true,
    your covenant remains constant.
You will never alter your promise to us.
You will never break your word.
Through your name,
    we lift our heads.
And in your name,
    we offer our prayer. Amen.

WORDS OF ASSURANCE (EPHESIANS 2)
You were far away.
But by the blood of Christ,
    you have been brought near.
In him, you are reconciled to God in one body,
    as members of the Lord's household.
In Christ, there is peace—
    peace to you who were faraway;
    peace to you who have been brought near!

BENEDICTION (EPHESIANS 2)
You're no longer strangers in a strange land.
You're now fellow-citizens with all of God's people!
You're the Lord's spiritual dwelling.
And Christ Jesus himself is the cornerstone!
Build this house together.
Be bonded together as members of God's household!
The Lord's presence lives within you!

JULY 30, 2006

Eighth Sunday after Pentecost
Judy Schultz

COLOR
Green

SCRIPTURE READINGS
2 Samuel 11:1-15; Psalm 14; Ephesians 3:14-21; John 6:1-21

THEME IDEAS
The story of David's temptation and sinful dalliance with the wife of Uriah the Hittite, reminds us of our own fallibility. And while David was guilty of great sin, he was also Israel's greatest king, and was deeply beloved of God. Sin does not end our relationship with God. Turning to the gospel reading, even if the sacrament is not celebrated, the story of Jesus feeding the five thousand can be linked to Holy Communion, for all who were fed by Jesus were satisfied. Connecting these narratives is the theme of being satisfied, not by what feeds our physical appetites, but by God, who satisfies the hungers of our hearts. From Ephesians we find the phrases "strengthened in your inner being" and being "rooted and grounded in love." Both are ideal themes for proclaiming to the church the life of the Body of Christ in the world.

CALL TO WORSHIP (PSALM 14)

Come and worship, people of God,
for God is with the righteous.
We come hungrily to worship,
but we know that we are not always righteous.
Come and worship, people of God,
for God is with the wise.
We come expectantly to worship,
but we know that we are not always wise.
Come and worship, people of God,
for God is with the needy.
We come longingly to worship,
for our need has brought us here today.
Come, let us worship God gratefully and joyfully!

CALL TO WORSHIP (JOHN 6)

From our busy lives, we have come into the presence
of the Holy God.
We come, hungry for God's word and Holy Spirit.
Even though summer is the time for vacations and
leisure, we stay busy people.
We come, that our work may not take over our lives.
We come, to feed our hungry spirits as well.
Here, in this place, we find an abundance of God's Spirit,
to satisfy our need.
Let us worship God together!

CALL TO WORSHIP

From the beauty of summer,
come into the sanctuary of God.
We come for rest and refreshment.
From the tension of our lives,
come into the sanctuary of God.
We come for inspiration and encouragement.
From the ordinariness of daily living,
come into the sanctuary of God.

We come, hoping to glimpse the holy
and to be transformed by it.
Let us worship God together!

CONTEMPORARY GATHERING WORDS (EPHESIANS 3)

Come, beloved of God, into this place of worship!
Come, beloved of God, into this place of praise!
Come, beloved people of God,
to raise our hands in praise,
and to bow our heads in prayer.
Come and worship, beloved people of God!

PRAISE SENTENCES

Our God is a wise God.
We come seeking God's wisdom.
Our God is a loving God.
We come seeking God's love.
Our God is a welcoming God.
We come seeking our spirits' home.

OPENING PRAYER (EPHESIANS 3, SUMMER)

Holy and loving God,
we come into your presence
on this morning in summer,
filled with the praises of your holy being.
You who created the mountains and lakes,
the great oceans and gentle rivers,
have given us a home for our refreshment.
Forgive us, O God,
when we become so busy with the details of our lives,
that we forget to look up and see your love
shouting to us in the world around us.
Into this beautiful garden world, O God,
help us to see your daily love, care,
and offer of renewal
for our souls. Amen.

OPENING PRAYER (EPHESIANS 3)

O holy God,
as the great trees reach up into the sky,
while rooted deeply in the earth,
so let our lives reach upwards to your spirit,
while rooted deeply in your love.
Help us so to live,
that through our words and actions,
others may see your spirit shining through us.
May your name be magnified through us,
and through your church universal. Amen.

UNISON PRAYER OR PRAYER OF CONFESSION (2 SAMUEL 11, JOHN 6)

Great God of heaven and earth,
in your love there is also accountability.
As you saw the actions of King David,
so you see our own.
And when we transgress,
it wounds your Holy Spirit.
Forgive us, we pray,
for all the times we take what is not ours,
for all the times we refuse to share,
for all the times we turn away from your loving spirit.
Forgive us, O God,
when we fail to choose life
for ourselves or for others. Amen.

WORDS OF ASSURANCE (2 SAMUEL 11, EPHESIANS 3)

As great as your love was to King David,
so great is your love also to us.
For you sent us your Son Jesus,
to give us life in your Spirit.
And in Jesus' life, death, and resurrection,
we are rooted in your love and forgiveness.
In the name of Jesus the Christ, you are forgiven.

BENEDICTION
Go now from this holy place,
   knowing you have been welcomed, loved, forgiven,
   and commissioned.
Go now from this place,
   knowing that you bear God's love to the world.
Bear that love joyfully and generously.
Let all who see your face,
   see the face of God.
Go in peace, and in joy. Amen!

BENEDICTION (EPHESIANS 3)
Go in peace.
Let God's love surround and center you,
   that those whom you meet may experience
   something of God's Spirit through your words
      and actions.
Go out joyfully,
   to love God and serve God's people. Amen.

AUGUST 6, 2006

Ninth Sunday after Pentecost
Bill Hoppe

COLOR
Green

SCRIPTURE READINGS
2 Samuel 11:26–12:13*a*; Psalm 51:1-12; Ephesians 4:1-16;
John 6:24-35

THEME IDEAS
In today's readings, we find trickery, craftiness, and
deceitful scheming (Ephesians 4:14). We learn that some
follow Jesus solely for their own benefit; some even follow
just for the loaves and fishes—the free food! King David is
confronted with the ugly truth that he has murdered Uriah
in order to take Uriah's wife, Bathsheba, with whom he
has already committed adultery, as his own. All sought to
satisfy their earthly desires. All sought satisfaction from
the food that perishes, rather than the food that endures
for eternal life (John 6:27). To their credit, all recognized
the error of their ways, no matter how great or small their
crimes. David repented of his grievous sin, accepting the
Lord's judgment. Jesus' freeloading followers asked him
for the bread of life. And even the psalmist asked God for
a clean heart. The apostle Paul ties things together as he
exhorts us to live lives worthy of the Lord's calling, in the
unity of the Spirit and in the bond of peace.

CALL TO WORSHIP (JOHN 6)

What must we do to perform the work of God?
This is the work: believe in the one sent by God!
What sign will be given, that we may see and believe?
**This is the sign: the bread of God comes down
from heaven!**
The bread of God gives life to the world!
Lord, give us this bread now!
Lord, give us this bread always!

CONTEMPORARY GATHERING WORDS
(2 SAMUEL 11)

David sinned against God.
He compounded his sin
    by trying to hide what he'd done.
He was exposed by the truth of God's word.
He confessed his sin.
He was forgiven.
He faced the consequences.
David worshiped the Lord.

PRAISE SENTENCES (EPHESIANS 4)

There is one body and one Spirit!
There is one hope, one calling!
There is one Lord, one faith, one baptism!
There is one God and Lord of all!

OPENING PRAYER (JOHN 6)

Gracious and merciful God,
    you sustain us.
You have given us
    the bread of heaven.
When we eat your bread,
    we are filled;
When we drink your cup,
    we are satisfied.

We will never hunger again.
We will never thirst again.
Gracious and merciful God,
   you sustain us. Amen.

OPENING PRAYER (EPHESIANS 4)

You have given each of us your gifts, Lord.
You have given us the bountiful grace of Christ.
Your gifts equip us for your ministry,
   growing and strengthening
      the Body of Christ.
Help us to grow.
Help us to mature,
   that your body may be built up
      in love. Amen.

PRAYER OF CONFESSION (PSALM 51)

My sin is against you
   and you alone, Lord.
You have exposed me for what I am.
All day long, I'm tormented by my sin.
You alone can cleanse me.
You alone can put away my shame.
Turn your face from my guilt, Lord.
Give me a new heart.
Give me a truthful spirit.
Keep me in your presence.
Heal my broken heart.
Return the joy of your salvation to me.
Help me remember the elation
   of your deliverance.
Uphold me by your Holy Spirit.
Hear my prayer.
Hear my cry
   in Jesus' name. Amen.

WORD OF ASSURANCE (PSALM 51)

You are washed; you are clean. The Lord has made you
whiter than snow.
Songs of joy and gladness will return.
Broken bones will be made to dance again.
Your sin fades in the light of forgiveness.
Your God has restored your soul.

PRAYER OF CONFESSION (JOHN 6, PSALM 51)

Though we labor for food that perishes, Lord,
    you will give us bread that endures forever.
Though we do what displeases you—
    you will show us mercy;
    you will forgive our sin.
Though the truth
    may be hidden in darkness, Lord,
    you will teach us wisdom.
Teach us; feed us; forgive us. Amen.

BENEDICTION (EPHESIANS 4)

The Lord has called you.
Live up to the call!
Be humble.
Be gentle and patient.
Spare no effort to love one another!
Speak the truth in love.
Grow in God's love!

AUGUST 13, 2006

Tenth Sunday after Pentecost
Mary Petrina Boyd

COLOR
Green

SCRIPTURE READINGS
2 Samuel 18:5-9, 15, 31-33; Psalm 130; Ephesians 4:25–5:2;
John 6:35, 41-51

THEME IDEAS
So many of our human efforts fail. Families and communities are torn apart by rebellion and violence. We nurture bitterness and anger and live with falsehood. Left to our own resources, we despair, but Jesus comes to us as the living bread, feeding our hungers, healing our wounds. God's steadfast love and power to redeem is greater than our human fears and deceits. In the incarnation, God is present in Jesus, even to the point of suffering and death. In the cross, God's power and love transform human violence into eternal life.

CALL TO WORSHIP (PSALM 130)
I wait for the Lord.
I trust in God's word.
My soul waits for the Lord.
Hope in the Lord!
With the Lord there is steadfast love.
With God there is great power to redeem.

CALL TO WORSHIP (JOHN 6)

We are hungry for God's word.
Jesus said, "I am the bread of life."
We long for God's love.
Jesus said, "I am the living bread."
We thirst for righteousness.
Jesus said, "I am the living water."
Come worship the Eternal One.
Come worship our Lord, Jesus Christ.

CALL TO WORSHIP (EPHESIANS 6)

Come Holy Spirit.
Mark us with the seal of your love.
Come Holy Spirit.
Give us tender, loving hearts.
Come Holy Spirit.
Show us how to forgive.
Come Holy Spirit.
Teach us to speak your truth.

CONTEMPORARY GATHERING WORDS (JOHN 6)

We are empty and our needs are great.
We are hungry for your peace.
Whoever comes to Jesus will never hunger.
We are thirsty for your word.
We long for the refreshment of grace.
Whoever believes in Christ will never thirst.

PRAISE SENTENCES (JOHN 6)

Jesus is the bread of life, the gift of God!
Jesus is the living bread, the promise of life eternal!

PRAISE SENTENCES (PSALM 130)

God has great power to redeem us!
God's love is steadfast!
God is our hope.

OPENING PRAYER (JOHN 6)

Bread of life,
    come and feed us—
        we hunger for your truth.
Living water,
    pour your grace upon us—
        we thirst for your righteousness.
Holy Christ,
    bring us eternal life. Amen.

OPENING PRAYER (PSALM 130)

We are waiting Lord:
    waiting for your call,
    waiting for your assurance,
    waiting for your peace.
We are waiting Lord:
    waiting for your love,
    waiting for your power,
    waiting for your presence.
We are your people:
    waiting for you,
    waiting in faith. Amen.

UNISON PRAYER (2 SAMUEL 18)

God of steadfast love,
    we live in a violent world.
Nations are at war.
Families rebel.
People nurture hatred and malice.
We grieve for those lost to violence—
    for the lives cut short,
    for broken relationships,
    for dreams destroyed.
We feel powerless against such great evil.
Come, O God,

surround us with your presence.
Work within our world
   to nurture tenderness, forgiveness,
   caring, and peace.
Show us your truth.
Redeem us, O Lord. Amen.

PRAYER OF CONFESSION (PSALM 130, EPHESIANS 4)
God of steadfast love,
   we so often fail you.
We nurture anger and violence,
   and fail to see that all people
      are your beloved children.
Our words are destructive
   and hurtful.
Teach us to imitate you.
May love and kindness
   spring up in our lives.
May we be tenderhearted
   and forgiving.
May our words bring healing
   and reconciliation. Amen.

WORDS OF ASSURANCE (PSALM 130)
God's love is steadfast.
God has the power to forgive us.

BENEDICTION (EPHESIANS 4)
Go as imitators of God.
Go as God's beloved children.
Live in love,
Rejoice in life
Be kind to one another. Amen.

BENEDICTION (JOHN 6, EPHESIANS 4)

We came hungry for God's word.
Jesus, the bread of life, feeds us.
We came thirsting for God's grace.
Jesus, the living water, revives us.
We go as God's people, beloved and free.
We go as God's people to serve the world.

AUGUST 20, 2006

Eleventh Sunday After Pentecost

B. J. Beu

COLOR
Green

SCRIPTURE READINGS
1 Kings 2:10-12; 3:3-14; Psalm 111; Ephesians 5:15-20; John 6:51-58

THEME IDEAS
Three of today's lections deal explicitly with wisdom and the benefits of wise behavior. In 1 Kings, Solomon, who inherits the throne as a mere youth, asks God for the understanding and wisdom necessary to lead God's people. The psalmist advises that "fear of the Lord is the beginning of wisdom." The epistle reading warns that unwise people prefer the intoxication of wine to being filled with the Holy Spirit. And while the gospel reading does not deal explicitly with wisdom, Jesus makes clear the wisdom of partaking of his body and blood to attain eternal life.

CALL TO WORSHIP (PSALM 111)
Praise the Lord!
God is our joy.
The Lord's works are a wonder to behold.
God's works are marvelous in our eyes.

The Lord is gracious and merciful.
God is faithful and just.
The Lord has brought redemption to God's people.
God's word is certain and true.
Fear of the Lord is the beginning of wisdom.
God leads us into life.
Praise the Lord!

CALL TO WORSHIP (EPHESIANS 5)

Be filled with the Spirit.
We are filled with the power of God's Holy Spirit.
Be filled with the Spirit.
We are filled with the glory of our God.
Be filled with the Spirit.
We are filled with the wisdom of Jesus, the Christ.

CONTEMPORARY GATHERING WORDS (PSALM 111)

Praise the Lord you people of God!
God's works are wonderful.
Praise the Lord you people of God!
God feeds and clothes us.
Praise the Lord you people of God!
God saves and sustains us.
Praise the Lord you people of God!
God's works are wonderful.
In fear and trembling, let us worship the Lord!

CONTEMPORARY GATHERING WORDS (JOHN 6)

The bread of heaven is here, leading us into life.
We live by the bread of life.
Christ's blood has been shed to bring us life.
We live by the cup of salvation.
Eat and drink. Christ brings us eternal life.
God gives us the body and blood of Christ.

PRAISE SENTENCES (PSALM 111)

Praise the Lord!
Praise the Lord of life!
Praise the Lord!
Praise the Lord of life!
Praise the Lord!
Praise the Lord of life!

PRAISE SENTENCES (1 KINGS 2)

Wisdom belongs to our God.
God, grant us wisdom.
Understanding belongs to our God.
God, grant us understanding.
Life belongs to our God.
God, grant us life.

OPENING PRAYER (JOHN 6)

Lord of life,
   you are the living bread
      that came down from heaven.
Give us this bread,
   that we may never hunger.
Lord of life,
   your blood redeems and saves us.
Give us life in your blood,
   that we may never thirst.
Lord of life,
   abide in us
      that we may abide in you.
Bring us into your kingdom
   which has no end. Amen.

OPENING PRAYER (1 KINGS 2)

Eternal God,
   your steadfast love endures forever.
When your servant David died,

leaving his throne to young Solomon,
you were there.
When Solomon sought the wisdom to rule your people,
and the understanding to discern good from evil,
you were there.
God, bestow your wisdom and discernment upon us,
that our judgments may be sound
and our decisions full of understanding. Amen.

BENEDICTION (1 KINGS 2, PSALM 111)

God, who is faithful, will grant us wisdom.
We go with the blessings of God,
who grants us wisdom.
God, who is faithful, will grant us understanding.
We go with the blessings of God,
who grants us understanding.
Go with God.

BENEDICTION (JOHN 6)

Christ has come to save us.
We are born anew.
The Spirit has come to save us.
We are born again.
Go with the blessings of Christ, who came,
not to condemn the world, but to save it.
We go with the blessings of Almighty God.

AUGUST 27, 2006

Twelfth Sunday after Pentecost
Christine S. Boardman

COLOR
Green

SCRIPTURE READINGS
1 Kings 8:(1, 6, 1-11) 22-30, 41-43; Psalm 84; Ephesians 6:10-20; John 6:56-69

THEME IDEAS
We are all captive to something or someone in our lives. Are we captive to rigid ideas or opinions that diminish others? Are we captive to fears that seem to offer only a fight or flight response? Does our past keep us confined, as we avoid facing the opportunities that may bring danger but are our only redemption as a people? Disciples in this century have an opportunity to bring our humanity to the holy dwelling place of the God of hosts, the God of gods. We are promised freedom to challenge what would keep us from being a loving, peaceful, forgiving, and hopeful people.

CALL TO WORSHIP (PSALM 84, EPHESIANS 6, JOHN 6)
What a pleasure and privilege it is to worship
in God's dwelling place—a place of refreshing springs

and of natural beauty, of safety, and of acceptance.
We are here to receive God's Spirit and life.
What an amazing covenant community we are as we find
shelter and solace, challenge and encouragement.
We are here to face our fears
and to sing of God's goodness.
What love God showers on us as we seek a home,
a relationship, and a life that exemplifies the gospel
of peace, hope, and freedom.
We are here to take our place
as we walk in the way of Jesus Christ.
The Holy One of God awaits our praise,
receives our allegiance, and blesses our lives.
Let us worship the God of hosts, the Holy One of God,
and the Spirit of life everlasting.

CALL TO WORSHIP (JOHN 6)

We wish for what we do not have!
What is it that we need?
We cry out for what would protect us!
What are we afraid of?
We long for what will free us!
Jesus is lord. Jesus leads us.
Jesus freed us to love.

CONTEMPORARY GATHERING WORDS (1 KINGS 8, PSALM 84, EPHESIANS 6)

This is the time and place for us to sing, think, feel,
and know God's presence in this community,
this holy dwelling place.
It is good to enter the gates of this place and rest awhile.
Look about, and know God is the strength and the support
that we crave above all else.
Now take a deep breath.
Now breathe out all that would keep you from being alert
here and now.

This is not simply a house made of our hands.
This is a holy place, the court of God's grace.

CALL TO WORSHIP (JOHN 6)
Jesus is Lord!
Jesus protects us from harm.
Jesus is Lord!
Jesus frees us to love.
Jesus is Lord!
Jesus is Lord! (B. J. Beu)

OPENING PRAYER (1 KINGS 8, PSALM 84)
Most gracious and loving God,
  we have gathered to worship together.
Open us fully to your presence
  as we come to this holy house
    of prayer and praise.
Speak to us.
Be present among us.
Share your vision for our church
  and for our individual lives.
Provide us a nest of your making,
  a spring of living waters that refreshes.
Help us to be open to our needs,
  our fears and our questions,
  that you may dwell with us
    as you have promised.
O God of all gods,
  may we receive all that we need
  in order to leave more certain and more ready
  to serve as disciples of Jesus. Amen.

PRAYER OF CONFESSION (JOHN 6)
God does not demand blood sacrifice from us.
Expect God to be merciful.
Let us speak these words of confession in one voice,
  that God's promise of mercy

may be fulfilled in our prayer.
Hear us now, O God of great wisdom and understanding.
In this house of prayer,
we thank you for your gracious leading.
We confess that it is a challenge
to know how to live as followers of Jesus.
We struggle sometimes.
When we are fearful or uncertain,
give us wisdom.
When we are defensive or even hostile
to interruptions and opportunities,
give us clarity and understanding.
When we act as if we lack what we need,
forgive us and inspire us with your Holy Presence.
We pray in the name of the One
who came to bring life and spirit to this world. Amen.

ASSURANCE OF PARDON (JOHN 6, EPHESIANS 6)
It is better to follow Jesus
than to be left behind
clinging to that which will never satisfy.
People of God, our gracious and forgiving God
is pleased that we have confessed our weakness.
In Christ we are made strong.

BENEDICTION (PSALM 84)
People of God,
let us now leave this holy dwelling place
to go out into this world as Christ's Body.
Let us depart as a body of the faithful,
ready to serve, support, and sing of God's goodness
and steadfast love.
People of God,
leave with the blessing of the God of hosts,
the Holy One of God, and the Spirit of life everlasting.
Amen.

SEPTEMBER 3, 2006

Thirteenth Sunday after Pentecost
Mary J. Scifres

COLOR
Green

SCRIPTURE READINGS
Song of Solomon 2:8-13; Psalm 45:1-2, 6-9 (or Psalm 72); James 1:17-27; Mark 7:1-8, 14-15, 21-23

THEME IDEAS
Love and joy abound in Solomon's Song and in Psalm 45, as humans find love for one another and Christians reflect on the love between Christ and the church. James echoes this theme of love in his letter, urging Christians to live the word of God through acts of love and giving, thereby responding to the messages we hear in Jesus' life and teachings. In Mark's gospel, Jesus gives us a poignant message for living—that the evil resting within our hearts is the most dangerous temptation of all. But within that warning is also a blessing—that the liberation from law and tradition permits us to live the good news out of love and gratitude, out of heartfelt commitment and faith.

CALL TO WORSHIP (PSALM 45)
My heart overflows with joy and love
as our church family gathers again.
Our hearts overflow with joy and love

as we worship together again.
God calls us to worship,
with hearts full of gladness.
We enter God's presence
with gratitude and praise.
Come, we are worshiping God!

CALL TO WORSHIP (SONG OF SOLOMON 2)
The voice of God is calling.
Our beloved Christ calls us here.
The voice of love is calling.
Our hearts of faith answer with joy.
Rise up and worship the Holy One.
We rise as beloved children of God.

CALL TO WORSHIP (SONG OF SOLOMON 2)
Arise, beloved, and come away.
Come into the presence of God.
Arise, beloved, and sing our God's praise.
Come into the presence of love.

CALL TO WORSHIP (JAMES 1)
All good gifts come from God above,
gifts of life and light and love.
The gift of worship and the gift of praise,
call to us this hour.
Let us worship the Giver of these gifts.

CALL TO WORSHIP OR RESPONSIVE READINGS (JAMES 1)
Let us be quick to listen and slow to speak.
Let us be gentle in spirit and slow to anger.
Let us welcome the word with humility and faith.
Let us welcome the word that saves our souls.
Let us live the word with faithfulness and love.
Let us live as disciples, enacting God's word.

CONTEMPORARY GATHERING WORDS (MARK 7)

Are you weary with burdens and unsure of your worth?
God is calling especially to you!
Are you tired of rules and overwhelmed with guilt?
God is calling especially to you!
Are you ready to live, ready to praise?
God is calling especially to you!
Are you ready to turn your hearts to Christ Jesus?
God is calling especially to you!

PRAISE SENTENCES (SONG OF SOLOMON 2)

Arise, people of God!
Arise and worship the Lord!
Arise, people of God!
Arise, and worship the Lord!

PRAISE SENTENCES (PSALM 45)

God's love is forever and ever!
God's love will never end.
God's love is forever and ever!
God's love will never end.

OPENING PRAYER (JAMES 1, MARK 7)

Father of lights and Mother of love,
    enter into our lives.
Shine through us with love and truth.
Guide us on this path of faith
    that we might honor you
        not only with our lips,
        but also with our lives.
Grant us the courage
    to live into your teachings
    and work for your justice.
Help us always and everywhere
    to be known as your disciples
        by all that we say
        and all that we do. Amen.

OPENING PRAYER (SONG OF SOLOMON 2, PSALM 45, JAMES 1)

Beloved God,
we praise you for inviting us
into your presence,
a presence of awesome holiness.
We thank you for your abundant love,
rich in mercy and grace.
We honor you for your steadfast faithfulness,
overflowing with passion and trust.
As we worship and pray,
enter into our hearts and our lives
that we may share with others
the same welcome and love and faithfulness
that you have shared with us. Amen.

PRAYER OF CONFESSION (JAMES 1)

Gracious God,
forgive us for living our lives
without the passion and purpose
you embodied in Christ Jesus.
When we settle into the comfortable position
of hearing your word
without living your word.
Forgive us and grant us mercy.
But do not let your mercy
end with forgiveness.
Call us forward into new life.
Pull us out of the darkness of complacency
and into the light of compassion and care.
Help us so to live as doers of the word
that all whom we meet are cared for
in their distress and laughed with
in their joy. Amen and amen.

PRAYER OF CONFESSION (MARK 7, JAMES 1)
O God of perfect love,
cleanse us of the many impurities
that haunt our minds and pollute our souls.
Create a new heart within each of us,
that we may be free of those evil things
that would defile us and limit our ministries
as your disciples in the world.
Help us to be quick to listen
and slow to speak.
Help us to be quick to forgive
and slow to anger.
Guide us on the path of humility and righteousness,
that we may guide others
into the truth of your love and compassion.
In the name of love, we pray. Amen.

WORDS OF ASSURANCE (SONG OF SOLOMON 2)
Arise, beloved children of God.
Look, Christ comes,
leaping down from heaven
to be in our midst.
Look again, Christ comes,
leaping with grace
to call us into new life.
Our lover God has spoken,
"Behold, I make all things new!"
Arise, beloved children of God.
You are made new
in the forgiveness of Christ.

BENEDICTION (JAMES 1)
Go forth as doers of the word.
Live as lovers of the world.
Care as caretakers of Christ's sheep.
And love as beloved children of God.

BENEDICTION (SONG OF SOLOMON 2)
Arise, beloved, and go forth.
We go into God's amazing world.
Arise, beloved, and share God's love.
We go forth with praise and joy.

SEPTEMBER 10, 2006

Fourteenth Sunday after Pentecost
Joanne Carlson Brown

COLOR
Green

SCRIPTURE READINGS
Proverbs 22:1-2, 8-9, 22-23; Psalm 125 (or Psalm 124); James 2:1-10 (11-13), 14-17; Mark 7:24-37

THEME IDEAS
Our God is an inclusive God and we are called to be inclusive as well. But God has a preferential option for the poor, the oppressed, and the outcast. We all need to be reminded of this, even Jesus. This is a day to help our congregations understand just how wide the gospel message is. This is a day to remember that we are called not only to believe, but to act on that belief, if we are to have a living, transforming faith.

CALL TO WORSHIP (PSALM 124)
Rejoice, people of God. God is on our side!
Blessed be God!
God has saved us from all harm!
Blessed be God!
Our help is in the name of God
who made heaven and earth.
Blessed be God forever!
Come, let us worship the God of our salvation.

CALL TO WORSHIP (PROVERBS 22)

Come, people of God. Come rich and poor alike.
God is the maker of us all.
Come and worship our generous God.
God calls us to share this abundance.
Come and worship the God who pleads our case.
**We worship with hearts and hands and voices
the God of all.**

CALL TO WORSHIP (JAMES 2)

Our God is a great and loving God.
We come to worship with our whole lives.
Our God calls us to love and serve everyone.
We will love our neighbor as ourselves.
Come and worship the God of faith and works.
We will worship God with a living, loving faith.

CONTEMPORARY GATHERING WORDS (JAMES 2, MARK 7)

God is here in this place, calling all God's children
to worship with their whole lives.
**We come, bringing our faith made alive
through works of love and mercy and liberation.**
Come, trusting that God will always respond to our need.
We come in trust and joy and faith and deeds.

PRAISE SENTENCES (PSALM 124)

Blessed be the God who is always on our side!
Praise to the God who rescues us from all evil!
Praise to our God in whom we find help and comfort
all of our days.

OPENING PRAYER (PSALM 124, PROVERBS 22)

O God,
we come this morning
seeking your presence.

Fill us with the knowledge
  of your work within us
  and within the world.
Help us remember
  that you are with us no matter what,
  that you are our Savior,
    a very present help in times of trouble.
May we claim our good name
  through our faith and deeds.
May we be blessed for showing your love
  to the last and the least. Amen.

OPENING PRAYER (JAMES 2)
God of all people,
  you call us to care for all people,
  especially for the poor and oppressed
    and marginalized.
Open our hearts and our hands
  to respond with generosity of spirit
    and of resources.
Help us to truly love our neighbor as ourselves.
May our deed and our faith
  always be one and the same,
  that all will know that we worship and serve
    a living, loving God. Amen.

PRAYER OF CONFESSION (MARK 7)
O God,
  we come with sighs too deep for words.
We find ourselves at times too self-centered.
We show partiality to those who are like us.
We fear and reject those who are foreign to us.
We close our ears to their cries
  and our hearts to their needs.
We do not even offer crumbs.
Help us to have a generous and open spirit.
May we always be willing to admit our mistakes

in judgment and in deed
and work to correct the injustices they may cause.
May we have a living faith
and transform us with your radical love,
that we may be the people you call us to be. Amen.

WORDS OF ASSURANCE (PSALM 124)

No matter what, God is always on our side,
ready to receive us and redeem us.
God will never abandon us.
Our help is in the One
who made heaven and earth.

BENEDICTION (PROVERBS 22)

Go forth, claiming your good name in word and deed.
We go forth, knowing that God is the maker of all.
Go forth with a generous spirit,
sharing the love of God with all people.
We go forth blessed by our generous God.
Go forth to be God's hands and feet in this world.
We go with joy, and in the strength
of our beloved God.

BENEDICTION (PROVERBS 22, PSALM 125, JAMES 2, MARK 7)

Go forth with the psalmist,
proclaiming God's steadfast and saving love.
Go forth with the writer of Proverbs,
in the sure knowledge of God's redeeming work.
Go forth with James,
claiming your heritage in works of faith.
And go forth with the Syrophoenician woman,
secure in the knowledge that no matter what,
you are a beloved child of God.

SEPTEMBER 17, 2006

Fifteenth Sunday after Pentecost

B. J. Beu

COLOR
Green

SCRIPTURE READINGS
Proverbs 1:20-33; Psalm 19; James 3:1-12; Mark 8:27-38

THEME IDEAS
While today's scriptures are not related thematically, a common thread may be found in Proverbs, James, and Mark: willful people do foolish and destructive things that greatly annoy God. In Proverbs, Wisdom cries out against those who love being simple and who are committed to folly. When calamity strikes, she will laugh, for we have all been duly warned. The epistle warns against the dangers of gossip and errant teachings, illustrating how the very fires of hell can be unleashed through the destructive power of an unbridled tongue. Finally, Mark's gospel highlights Peter's big mistake in rebuking Jesus. Peter himself is rebuked for setting his mind on worldly rather than divine things. The psalmist, however, moves us in another direction entirely, joyfully proclaiming that the heavens declare God's glory.

CALL TO WORSHIP (PSALM 19)
The Heavens are telling the glory of God.
The firmament proclaims God's handiwork.

197

The sun rises like a bridegroom to meet the day.
Earth and sky sing God's praises.
The law of the Lord is perfect, reviving the soul.
The precepts of God are sweet as honey.
Let us shout praises to our God.
Let us sing praises to God's glory.
Let us join the heavens and tell of God's glory.

CALL TO WORSHIP (PROVERBS 1)
Wisdom cries out to us.
When will we listen?
We will not shut out the lessons she teaches.
Wisdom cries out to us.
How long will we scoff?
We will not shut out the lessons she teaches.
Wisdom cries out to us.
How long will we hate knowledge?
We will not shut out the lessons she teaches.
Wisdom cries out to us.
Fear of the Lord is the beginning of wisdom.
We have come to worship God and to listen.

CONTEMPORARY GATHERING WORDS (MARK 8)
Jesus asks: "Who do others say that I am?"
You are a prophet, sent by God.
"But who do you say that I am?"
You are the Messiah, the blessed one of God.
"Will you pick up your cross and follow me?"
Isn't there an easier way?
"Can you set your minds on heavenly things
for a change?"
We want to follow you.
"Come and follow, I will help you carry your burdens."
Thanks be to God!

CONTEMPORARY GATHERING WORDS (PSALM 19)

Can you hear the heavens?
They proclaim God's glory.
Can you hear the heavens?
They sing the majesty of God.
Can you sing like the heavens?
We have come to learn the song.
Let us sing God's praises together.

PRAISE SENTENCES (PSALM 19)

Sing God's praises with the heavens.
Sing God's praises with the sun.
Sing God's praises with the moon and stars.
Our God is worthy to be praised!

PRAISE SENTENCES (PROVERBS 1)

God's Wisdom is wonderful.
    She leads us into the fullness of life.
    God's Wisdom is wonderful.
She leads us into the fullness of life.

OPENING PRAYER OR PRAYER OF CONFESSION (MARK 8)

Loving Christ,
    you came into our world
        that we might set our minds on heavenly things.
We confess that we easily lose focus,
    turning our gaze to human concerns
    and earthly matters.
We are quick to declare who others say that you are,
    but are slow to make public
    our own declarations of faith.
Help us have Peter's vision to see you as our Messiah,
    but save us from personal agendas
        that seek to create you anew in our image
        of what a savior should be.

Teach us to follow the hard road,
that others may meet us on the journey,
and through us, discover you. Amen.

OPENING PRAYER OR PRAYER OF CONFESSION (JAMES 3)

Holy God,
teach us to see ourselves
as we really are.
Bridle our lips,
that we might be spared
the temptation to gossip.
Yoke our desires,
that no evil may be done
through our actions.
May we,
who celebrate God's image in ourselves,
not curse others,
who also share God's image.
Grant us self-control,
that we might yield good fruit
in all that we do,
through Jesus Christ
who guides and strengthens us. Amen.

ASSURANCE OF PARDON (PSALM 19)

God is our rock and our redeemer,
our certain hope in times of trial.
We, who fall short of the glory of God,
are forgiven in Christ.
Seek the perfect law of God,
which is sweeter than honey,
and find forgiveness and redemption.

BENEDICTION (PROVERBS 1)

God's Wisdom leads us forth.
We rejoice in her teachings.

God's wisdom saves us from folly.
We rejoice in her teachings.
God's Wisdom leads us to care for one another.
We rejoice in her teachings.

BENEDICTION (MARK 8)

Christ offers us life.
Christ is our life.
Christ shows us God's glory.
Christ is our life.
Christ is the way of salvation.
Christ is our life.
Go with Christ's blessings.

SEPTEMBER 24, 2006

Sixteenth Sunday after Pentecost
Mary Petrina Boyd

COLOR
Green

SCRIPTURE READINGS
Proverbs 31:10-31; Psalm 1; James 3:13–4:3, 7-8a; Mark 9:30-37

THEME IDEAS
Today's scriptures center on our daily life, our work, and our service to others. They show how faith can be expressed in ordinary acts. The capable woman provides for her family and her community, building a life of faith rooted in the realities of daily life. Psalm 1 demonstrates the blessing found by those who root their lives in God. James confronts the reality of human strife and disagreement, and points to the higher wisdom, where grace fills life. Jesus recognizes the all too human desire for prestige, and lifts up love of a child as an example of God's realm. All this calls us to follow the ways of wisdom, which bring comfort and life to our world.

CALL TO WORSHIP (PROVERBS 31, JAMES 3–4)
Come, rest from your daily work.
Come and worship God.
Come, leave the worries of life.
Come and find peace.

Come, enter this place of worship.
Be nourished by God's love.

CALL TO WORSHIP (PROVERBS 31)

Our hands reach out to you.
Show us the work we must do.
Our hands reach out to you.
Show us the people we should serve.
Our hands reach out to you.
Embrace us with your love.

CALL TO WORSHIP (PSALM 1, PROVERBS 31, JAMES 3–4)

Let us delight in God's word,
for God gives us work to do.
Let us delight in God's word,
for God shows us how to serve.
Let us delight in God's word,
for God will make us fruitful.
Let us draw near to God,
as God draws near to us.

CONTEMPORARY GATHERING WORDS (PSALM 1)

Like clear, cool water,
God quenches our thirst.
Like a wise guide,
God shows us the way of the righteous.
Come and worship.
Sing praise and rejoice!

CONTEMPORARY GATHERING WORDS (PSALM 1, JAMES 3–4)

Come from the work of the world.
God's love is in this place.
Come from places of strife.
God's peace is in this place.
Come as you are to God.
God will show us the way.

PRAISE SENTENCES (PSALM 1)
Happy are those who walk in God's path.
God shows them the way.
Happy are those who stand in God's presence.
God refreshes their souls.
Happy are those who sit before God.
God gives them all that they need.

PRAISE SENTENCES (PROVERBS 31)
We won't worry about tomorrow,
for God always cares for us!
We laugh and rejoice today,
for God is here with us!

OPENING PRAYER (PSALM 1)
Like trees thirsting for water,
    our hearts long for you, O God.
In your presence
    we find life.
Nourish us in this time of worship,
that we may yield fruits of righteousness
    and justice in the world. Amen.

OPENING PRAYER (MARK 9)
We come as your children,
    eager to hear your word,
    longing for your presence.
May your arms of welcoming love
    embrace us in this hour.
Fill us with your wisdom
    and teach us understanding. Amen.

UNISON PRAYER (PROVERBS 31)
God of our days,
    you call us to work in your world.
Strengthen our arms

and encourage our hearts
    for the tasks you lay before us.
Help us to lay aside our worries
    and to rejoice in your gifts.
Silence our conflicts
    and teach us gentleness and mercy.
May all we do, praise you forever. Amen.

UNISON PRAYER (PROVERBS 31)

God, we are your people.
Transform us and make us anew.
Spin us into strong threads
    of love and caring.
Weave us into a community
    of wisdom and compassion,
    kindness and rejoicing.
Sew us into garments
    of strength and dignity.
We are your people,
    the work of your hands.
Let us praise you forever. Amen.

UNISON PRAYER (PSALM 1, JAMES 3–4)

God, you are the gardener,
    gently cultivating the soil of our lives,
    giving us water and life.
Thank you for all you give us,
    for your Spirit that nurtures us,
    bring life and strength.
May we bear the fruits of righteousness,
    gentleness, kindness, and peace.
May we be gentle and forgiving,
    turning away from anger,
    working for peace,
    rejoicing in each other's gifts. Amen.

PRAYER OF DEDICATION (PROVERBS 31)

Lord, you give us work to do.
As we live faithfully,
we find that you fill our lives with blessing.
With grateful hearts, we come to you,
bearing the fruits of our labors.
Use our gifts
to bring comfort and strength
to those in need.
Use us as your hands,
reaching out with compassion. Amen.

BENEDICTION (PSALM 1)

God has blessed you.
The waters of bounty restore us.
God has blessed you.
The paths of God's love lead us to life.
Go forth with joy, to live in God's ways.
We go with joy, to embrace God's world.

BENEDICTION (MARK 9)

Go out and do God's work.
Go out and love God's children.
Go out with God's blessing,
rejoicing in God's good gifts.

BENEDICTION (PSALM 1, JAMES 3–4)

May the wisdom of God rest upon you.
May the waters of God's love nourish you.
May the peace of God be yours,
today and every day.

OCTOBER 1, 2006

Seventeenth Sunday after Pentecost
World Communion Sunday

Laura Jaquith Bartlett

COLOR

Green

SCRIPTURE READINGS

Esther 7:1-6, 9-10; 9:20-22; Psalm 124; James 5:13-20; Mark 9:38-50

THEME IDEAS

Today's scriptures are full of sound advice. The Esther story ends with a model for how one culture will remember its heritage of God's saving grace in history. The James text offers a brief but excellent primer on the benefits of prayer. And the Mark reading has Jesus chastising the disciples for putting up obstacles to those who were not members of the "in crowd," ending with advice to be salty, and to be at peace with one another. What wonderful counsel for World Communion Sunday! Today, as we seek to join our prayers with Christians from cultures around the globe, it is helpful to remember that we are not the "in crowd" for the entire world. Let us come to worship together, with Jesus' words ringing in our ears: "Be at peace with one another."

CALL TO WORSHIP (ESTHER 7, WORLD COMMUNION)

From the ends of the earth,
God calls us together.
Blessed be the God of all nations!
From ancient times to modern times,
God calls us together.
Blessed be the God of all nations!
Young and old, leaders and followers,
God calls us together.
Blessed be the God of all nations!

CALL TO WORSHIP (WORLD COMMUNION)

(Other languages may be substituted or added, depending on what languages are represented in your congregation. Ideally, each sentence would be read by a native speaker. The congregational response should be printed in the native language of the congregation.)

Reader 1 (English)	Come, let us praise God together.
Reader 2 (Spanish)	Viene, alabemos Dios juntos.
Reader 3 (Korean)	Da Hamke Ju Chan-yang Hap-si-Da.
Reader 4 (German)	Kommen Sie, lassen Sie uns loben Gott zusammen.
Congregation	**Come, let us praise God together!**

CALL TO WORSHIP (WORLD COMMUNION)

God's love is at work in our church.
God's love is at work in our neighborhood.
God's love is at work in our community.
God's love is at work in our state.
God's love is at work in our nation.
God's love is at work in our world!

CONTEMPORARY GATHERING WORDS (MARK 9)

We're looking for salty folks!
Hey, what is this? Some sort of off-beat restaurant?

Well, food's on the menu today,
but it's not what you think.
We're hungry for food that will fill us up.
Come and eat! God offers food to fill your souls.
Praise God! There's room at the table for everyone.

PRAISE SENTENCES (PSALM 124, JAMES 5)

Blessed be the Lord.
Our help is in the name of the Lord,
 who made heaven and earth.
Blessed be the Lord.
Prayers of faith will save the sick,
 and the Lord will raise them up.
Blessed be the Lord.
The Lord has turned sorrow into gladness.
Blessed be the Lord.

OPENING PRAYER (WORLD COMMUNION)

Gracious God,
 we join with Christians around the world
  to glorify your name,
   singing songs of praise in every language.
As we share the bread and the cup of Holy Communion,
 we also share together in the Body of Christ.
Gathering around the table,
 we embody the vision of all God's children
  included at the same table.
We pray that our worship today
 will quicken the coming of your kingdom here on earth.
We pray for that glorious day
 when all who claim Christ as savior
  will proclaim our relationship together
   as sisters and brothers,
    bound together as the family of God.
Let every color, every nation, and every person
 join in singing, "Alleluia and Amen!"

OPENING PRAYER (JAMES 5, WORLD COMMUNION)

God of all the nations,
we know that there are people who are suffering,
around the world and in our midst.
Be with everyone who needs your healing touch.
Help us to have the faith of Elijah,
that we might pray without ceasing
for all persons in need.
Join our prayers with those of the faithful
in every corner of your creation.
And in the unity of our prayer, O God,
help us to be at peace with one another. Amen.

PRAYER OF CONFESSION (JAMES 5, MARK 9, WORLD COMMUNION)

Merciful God,
you call us to love one another,
but we object if people show their love
in ways that are foreign to us.
You call us to be at peace with one another,
but we forget that peace without justice
is only oppression.
You call us to care for one another,
but we would rather retreat
into our gated communities
and our cloistered sanctuaries.
Help us to recover the saltiness of being truly Christian.
On this World Communion Sunday,
we pray that we will know you
in the breaking of the bread,
that you offer to us all.
In the breaking of this bread,
may the barriers of cultural arrogance and prejudice
also be broken.
We pray in the name of the One who was broken for us,
your Son, Jesus Christ. Amen.

WORDS OF ASSURANCE (GALATIANS 3:28, WORLD COMMUNION)

There is no longer Jew or Greek.
There is no longer slave or free.
There is no longer male and female.
All of us are one in Christ Jesus.

BENEDICTION (WORLD COMMUNION)

May the love of God,
    offered for all the world's peoples,
        go with each of you today.
May the light of Christ,
    shining for all the world's peoples,
        be a beacon in your life today.
May the unity of the Spirit,
    binding together all the world's peoples,
        strengthen and comfort you today.

BENEDICTION (MARK 9)

Go now to be salty Christians!
Pray, sing, show love, and support one another.
In the name of Christ Jesus,
    go and be peacemakers in this world of strife.

OCTOBER 8, 2006

Eighteenth Sunday after Pentecost
Crystal R. Sygeel

COLOR
Green

SCRIPTURE READINGS
Job 1:1, 2:1-10; Psalm 26 (or Psalm 25); Hebrews 1:1-4, 2:5-12; Mark 10:2-16

THEME IDEAS
In all of these texts there is the theme of connectedness and the desire to stay in relationship. Whether between people, or between God and people, a message emerges: once a relationship has been established, one should not sever the relationship when something goes wrong. Job refuses to curse God despite his misfortunes, David calls to God in hopes of an answer, Paul assures the Hebrews of God's desire to connect with us through God's Son Jesus, and Jesus himself speaks of what it means to make a connection with another person in holy matrimony. The connections that exist between people, and between people and God, are not to be taken lightly or discarded at the first sign of trouble.

CALL TO WORSHIP (PSALM 26)
Come into God's presence.
Sing praises of joy!
We come with our songs and stories of faith.

Come into Christ's house.
Tell of God's wonderful deeds.
We love this house, full of mercy and grace.
Enter with the Spirit,
the Holy presence of God.
Blessings to the One who calls us here!
(Mary J. Scifres)

CALL TO WORSHIP (HEBREWS 1–2)

God speaks to us, through worship and words.
God calls to us, through space and time.
Come into the presence of God! (Mary J. Scifres)

CALL TO WORSHIP (HEBREWS 1–2)

The God of glory and grace welcomes you here.
What are humans that God notices us?
The God of faith and hope trusts in you.
How can God's image exist in us?
The God of love and life honors you now.
But we come to glorify God.
Let us praise this great God who loves us so.
We will praise you with our very lives.
(Mary J. Scifres)

CONTEMPORARY GATHERING WORDS (MARK 10)

Come in! Come in to worship!
Do you struggle with life?
Are your relationships full of challenges
    and complications?
The God of love is waiting for you!
Are your relationships full of pushes and pulls?
The God of reconciliation is waiting for you!
Are your relationships full of blessings and beauty?
The God of love is waiting for you!
Come in! Come in to worship!

CONTEMPORARY GATHERING WORDS (HEBREWS 1–2, MARK 10)

Praise the God who spoke to the prophets and the saints.
Praise the God who speaks to us today!
Praise the God who pursued our ancestors.
Praise the God who pursues us still!
Praise the God who crafted the faithful together.
Praise the God who weaves us together today!
Praise the God who united the saints in holy love.
Praise the God who weaves us together still!

PRAISE SENTENCES (HEBREWS 1–2)

Glory to God. Glory to Christ!
Glory to God in the highest!
Glory to God. Glory to Christ!
Glory to God in the highest!

OPENING PRAYER (HEBREWS 1–2)

God of covenant and connection,
we come into your courts
with hands outstretched.
With one hand
we reach across the earth
to your people.
With one hand
we reach across the cosmos
to you. Amen.

OPENING PRAYER (MARK 10)

Great Creator of Earth, Great Weaver of People,
show us your will for our relationships.
Show us how to connect with one another
in loving and gentle ways.
Show us how to be close to others,
without losing ourselves.
Show us how we are united as one,
yet remain unique. Amen.

PRAYER OF CONFESSION (JOB 1, PSALM 26, HEBREWS 1–2, MARK 10)
Holy God,
   there is something about connecting with those we love,
   the sense of something holding us together—
   invisible strings, silent songs echoing back and forth;
   one cord, with one person on each end.
But when disagreement creeps in
   and we enter into conflict—
      how the ropes tighten;
      how the notes become strained.
We are tempted to cut the ribbons that bind us together.
Help us remember that we are created
   to reflect your image.
Help us recall that the reward comes from holding on—
   from saying to others,
   "I am not like you, but I am with you";
   "I do not agree with you, but I am still here,
   connected to you."
God of Conflict, God of Reconciliation,
   prepare us for the discomfort of disagreement.
Let us hold fast to the ties that bind us together.
In our anxiety, let us twist and adjust,
   but give us the endurance to never let go. Amen.

WORDS OF ASSURANCE (HEBREWS 2, MARK 10)
Sisters and brothers, hear the good news!
Christ has died and Christ has risen.
In Christ all relationships are made new.
In Jesus Christ, you are forgiven!

BENEDICTION (HEBREWS 2)
Since we have a Savior, a perfect example of faith,
   we are able to take Christ to the world.
Since we know of God's mercy, perfect love and grace,
   we are able to live lives of love.

Since the Spirit is living within our own lives,
we are one with Christ Jesus our Lord.
Take courage, my friends! God has crowned us
with honor, and trusts us to live out Christ's love!
(Mary J. Scifres)

BENEDICTION (MARK 10)
And now go forward into this day,
 with a renewed commitment
  to all of your relationships.
Go forward into this day,
 with one hand reaching out to the world,
  and one hand reaching always to God! Amen.

OCTOBER 15, 2006

Nineteenth Sunday after Pentecost
Robert Blezard

COLOR
Green

SCRIPTURE READINGS
Job 23:1-9, 16-17; Psalm 22:1-15; Hebrews 4:12-16; Mark 10:17-31

THEME IDEAS
Life is sometimes very hard. Like Job, we can feel that we do not deserve our misfortunes in life, and we may yearn for a "hearing" before God. Surely a just God will lift the burdens from us. Other times, we feel like the writer of the psalm—that God has abandoned us altogether in our most desperate hour. But the good news is that Jesus understands our weaknesses and will reward us for the hardships we suffer for the sake of the gospel.

CALL TO WORSHIP (HEBREWS 4)
Let us approach the throne of grace with boldness.
The word of God is living and active.
Jesus sympathizes with our weaknesses.
The word of God is sharper than a sword.
We will find mercy and help in our time of need.
The word of God judges the intentions of our hearts.

CALL TO WORSHIP (MARK 10, HEBREWS 4)

With God, all things are possible!
There is hope for us.
Let us boldly approach the throne of grace.
**There, we receive help and mercy
in our time of need.**

CALL TO WORSHIP (PSALM 22)

When we cry out, "Where is our God?"
Jesus understands our weakness.
When we are frightened and are in great pain,
Jesus understands our weakness.
When enemies surround us and we feel so alone,
**Jesus understands our weakness,
and gives us help in our times of need.**

CONTEMPPORARY GATHERING WORDS (PSALM 22, HEBREWS 4)

Has anybody here not known pain?
Not felt abandoned by family and friends?
Felt abandoned even by God?
Life can be unbearably painful.
But God is always with us.
God helps us in our lives.

PRAISE SENTENCES (HEBREWS 4, MARK 10)

All things are possible with you, O God.
We raise our voices to you.
You hold us in your saving hand.
You give us help in times of need.

OPENING PRAYER (PSALM 22, HEBREWS 4)

O God of love and mercy,
we your children long for your parental arms
that enfold us to make us feel safe.
We long for your wisdom and advice

to guide our decisions.
We yearn for your unconditional love
 that emboldens us to live each day.
In our pain and brokenness,
 we cry out to you.
When we cannot feel your presence,
 help us find comfort in the promise
 that you will never abandon us.
Help us see that you are ready
 to shower us with you grace and your aid. Amen.

OPENING PRAYER (MARK 10)

Holy God,
 show us your ways,
 and give us the courage to choose
  the harder paths you lay before us
  in our walk as your disciples.
As we embrace charity for others,
 and poverty for ourselves,
  strengthen our resolve.
Help us to remember
 the grace that sustains us.
Give us your courage
 and your strength, O God.
Mold us into the people
 you want us to become. Amen.

PRAYER OF CONFESSION (MARK 10)

Most merciful God,
 Jesus teaches us that it is more difficult
  for a wealthy person to enter your kingdom,
  than it is for a camel to go through the eye
  of a needle.
Too often we have been blinded by the glitter of gold
 and sought to acquire more money and possessions
  than we need.

In our selfishness, we have ignored your call
to share our bounty with the poor in our midst,
choosing instead to walk away from the needy
in guilty sadness.
We beg your mercy and forgiveness.
We await your strength
and guidance to do better. Amen.

WORDS OF ASSURANCE (MARK 10)
Who can be saved?
Hear Jesus' words of comfort:
"For mortals it is impossible, but not for God.
For God, all things are possible."

BENEDICTION (HEBREWS 4)
May God, who hears every cry,
who answers every prayer,
who became incarnate through Jesus the Christ,
bless you and give you grace in times of need.

BENEDICTION (MARK 10)
Go in peace, with the love of our merciful God
for whom all things are possible!

OCTOBER 22, 2006

Twentieth Sunday after Pentecost
Jamie Greening

COLOR
Green

SCRIPTURE READINGS
Job 38:1-7 (34-41); Psalm 104:1-9, 24, 35c; Hebrews 5:1-10;
Mark 10:35-45

THEME IDEAS
Season themes collide with textual themes in these rich
passages about creation. The verdant themes of creation,
seasons, God's beauty, and dominion are emphasized.
Doctrinal themes of the sovereignty of God, creation,
doubting, provision, atonement, servant leadership, and
the cross can easily flow from these passages. Two of the
texts specifically emphasize the social issues of the envi-
ronment, and the fall season is a good time to think about
such issues. Or, another concept can be emphasized: the
difference between secular and sacred leadership, and
what this means in the church.

CALL TO WORSHIP (PSALM 104)
Let us praise the Lord.
With our souls we praise the Lord.
The Lord alone is great.
With our hearts we praise the Lord.

Let us praise the Lord.
Alleluia, alleluia.

CALL TO WORSHIP (JOB 38)

Pleiades and Orion are yours, O God.
So too, are we.
You alone have dominion.
You alone are Lord.
You bring seasonal rains.
Your Spirit moistens our hearts.
You have provided for our every need.
We give you thanks, O God.

CONTEMPORARY GATHERING WORDS (PSALM 104)

O Lord, your works are many.
We celebrate your wisdom.
Alleluia, alleluia.
We live by your light.
We worship in your sanctuary.
Alleluia, alleluia.

CONTEMPORARY GATHERING WORDS (JOB 38)

Yahweh laid the cornerstone of creation.
We celebrate the cornerstone.
Christ is the cornerstone of the church.
We celebrate the cornerstone.

PRAISE SENTENCES (JOB 38)

The Lord is the creator of heaven and earth.
In our humanity, we tremble at God's greatness.
Let us praise God's name for the wonders of creation.
Let us praise God's name for the sun, moon, and stars.
Let us praise God's name for hills, trees, birds, fish,
 and all the animals.
Let us praise God's name for giving the law
 and sending our Lord Jesus Christ.
Let us praise God's name for the promise of eternity.

PRAISE SENTENCES (MARK 10)

Praise be unto Jesus Christ,
> who alone could drink the cup of agony
> > that brings salvation.

Praise be unto Jesus Christ,
> who alone endured the baptism of pain.

Praise be unto Jesus Christ,
> who alone sits at the mighty right hand
> > of God the Father.

Praise be unto Jesus Christ,
> who alone provides the way to eternal life.

OPENING PRAYER (PSALM 104)

Lord,
> your greatness is evident in the sun,
> > sky, mountains and seas.

The wind, rain, thunder, and lightning bolts
> remind us of our great power.

Because of these and so much more,
> you are worthy to be praised.

We join with all of creation today
> to exalt your name. Amen. Alleluia.

UNISON PRAYER (HEBREWS 5)

We give thanks with one voice
> to our great high priest,
> > the Lord Jesus Christ. Amen.

UNISON PRAYER (MARK 10)

Teach us, Jesus,
> to live as servants.

Teach us Jesus,
> to serve each other.

Teach us Jesus,
> to abide in your ways—
> > in humility and meekness,

with compassion and empathy,
without pride or boastfulness,
and with a smile.
Teach us to do unto others,
as if we were doing unto you. Amen.

BENEDICTION (MARK 10)
We depart now to your service.
Help us serve one another.
Let us not seek to be first,
But instead seek to help.

BENEDICTION (PSALM 104, MARK 10)
May the security of the Lord's dominion
comfort each of us as we enter the world
to love and serve.

OCTOBER 29, 2006

Twenty-first Sunday after Pentecost
Reformation Sunday

Mark Dowdy

COLOR
Green

SCRIPTURE READINGS
Job 42:1-6, 10-17; Psalm 34:1-8 (19-22); Hebrews 7:23-28; Mark 10:46-52

THEME IDEAS
One of the themes of the Reformation is "Reformed, yet always reforming!" The reformers of old, both Protestant and Catholic, spoke truth to power and thereby helped change the way their communities thought about, and lived out, their faith. Those of our culture and communities who speak truth to power do similarly. Biblical reformers such as Job and Bartimaeus also helped their world and ours understand that God is always about the business of "re-forming" God's people. They stood up for their beliefs and made known their desires. God responded, and reformed their lives. May God continue to reform ours as well!

INVITATION TO WORSHIP (PSALM 34:1-8)

Leader   I will bless God at all times.
God's praise shall continually be in my mouth.

Men   **My soul makes its boast in God.**
Let the humble hear and be glad.

Leader   O magnify God with me, and let us exalt
God's name together.

Women   **I sought God, who answered me,**
and delivered me from all my fears.

Leader   Look to God, and be radiant.
Your face shall never be ashamed.
The angel of God encamps around those
who revere God and delivers them.

All   **O taste and see that God is good.**
Happy are those who take refuge in God.
Let us worship!

From The New Testament and Psalms: An Inclusive Version

CONTEMPORARY CALL TO WORSHIP (JOB 42)

Have you friends like Job, who harass and challenge?
We do, but know, like Job, that God can do
all things!
Can you approach God like Job, and challenge God
to listen?
We can! With as much determination and resolution
as Job.
Then, God isn't finished with you?
Not on your life! God isn't finished with us yet.
So let's sing praises and pray, and hear God's word
of reform this day!

OPENING PRAYER (HEBREWS 7)

Jesus our high priest,
we thank you that unlike those before you,
your sacrifice of faithfulness to death
was freely offered, once for all.

We thank you for praying for us
and for bringing us the guidance, health, forgiveness,
and new life we seek.
As you touch our lives
through the Word and through the Spirit,
may we continue to be reformed,
and ever formed anew. Amen.

UNISON PRAYER OR PRAYER OF CONFESSION (MARK 10:46-52)

Like blind Bartimaeus,
we long for sight and insight.
Like shy Bartimaeus,
we softly cry out as part of the crowd,
"Son of David, have mercy on me."
Have mercy on us, O God,
for the blindness in our lives.
Have mercy on us
for failing to recognize you
in the "other."
Have mercy on us
for not "seeing" our own blind spots,
prejudices, and biases.
Have mercy on us and heal us,
Son of David, God's anointed! Amen.

ASSURANCE OF PARDON (MARK 10)

Jesus heard and healed Bartimaeus.
The good news this day is that Jesus hears
and heals us too.
Bartimaeus left his old life and followed.
The good news is that God has had mercy on us
and we are forgiven!
Thanks be to God!

INVITATION TO SHARE GOD'S GIFTS (JOB 42, PSALM 34, MARK 10)

Like Job, we have a hard time understanding God's ways,
    yet know God is faithful.
Like the psalmist, we are joyful
    when we come through hard times
    and have confirmed that God is faithful.
Like Bartimaeus, we follow Jesus,
    having been touched by Christ.
May we be ever grateful.
And may we give out of that gratitude!

BENEDICTION (PSALM 34)

May the God who rescues us from afflictions
go with us into the world.
    May God go with us indeed!
May the God who keeps all our bones safe
be with us as we leave this holy place.
    May God be with us indeed!
May the God who redeems the lives of God's servants
continue to form and reform us!
    May God form and reform us indeed!
    And may we all go in peace! Amen.

NOVEMBER 1, 2006

All Saints Day

Bryan Schneider-Thomas

COLOR
White

SCRIPTURE READINGS
Isaiah 25:6-9; Psalm 24; Revelation 21:1-6*a*; John 11:32-44

THEME IDEAS
All Saints is a day to celebrate and give thanks for the community of faith and the individuals who comprise it, especially those who have passed into glory in the past year. The texts invite us to meditate on the kingdom of God. The kingdom of God, of which we are a part, in heaven and on earth, may be characterized in many ways—a lavish feast, a joyful celebration, a new city, a place of life. Today we celebrate the citizens of God's kingdom. Isaiah's opening words invite us to the celebration of communion—a foretaste of the feast to come.

CALL TO WORSHIP (ISAIAH 25)
On the mountain of God, we are invited to a rich feast:
 a feast of lavish foods and fine drink;
a feast for all people;
 a feast of triumph for our God.
And on that day we will say:
 This is our God, for whom we have waited.
 God will save us.

CALL TO WORSHIP (EPHESIANS 4, REVELATION 21)

We are one.
Throughout the ages, from beginning to end,
Jesus has made us one.
We are one.
One in Jesus; for there is one Lord, one faith,
and one baptism that unites us all.
We are one.
In life and death, God keeps us together,
for Jesus has destroyed death.
We are one.
Though we are many, we are one forevermore.

CONTEMPORARY GATHERING WORDS (JOHN 11)

Jesus stands before the tomb of a beloved friend.
"Roll the stone away" he says.
Let the dead man arise to new life. And Jesus says:
"Unbind him, and set him free."
Jesus stands before our tombs,
where we are bound in shrouds of death.
Let the dead arise to new life. And Jesus says:
"Unbind them, and set them free."
Through the saints that have gone before,
we know the promises of new life are for us as well.
Jesus' words speak clear to us.
"Unbind us, and set us free."
With Jesus' words still fresh in our hearing,
let us proclaim his promise to those we meet
who are still shrouded by death:
"Christ unbinds you, and sets you free."

PRAISE SENTENCES (ALL SAINTS)

God destroys all boundaries and calls us
    to celebrate with all people.
Through the church's saints, we learn the faith
    and join in praise.

By the grace of God shared through the faith of our
saints, we receive new life.
Behold, the kingdom is in our midst.

OPENING PRAYER (ISAIAH 25)

Holy God,
you are ever present.
We live in the shadows of the valley,
desiring to rise to glory,
but shrouded in worries, threats,
and fears.
Draw away the shroud,
and raise us up to the mountain peaks,
where we may join together
with all people in your glory.
Call us to the feast you have prepared,
that we may join in joyful praise. Amen.

OPENING PRAYER (REVELATION 21)

O Christ who is both beginning and end,
you chose to dwell with us
that we might be your people.
You have promised to be the end
of death, pain, and mourning.
You are the beginning of a new creation.
May we gather with all the church's saints
in singing your praises,
and glorifying your name. Amen.

OPENING PRAYER (JOHN 11)

God of all,
by you we have been given life,
and in you we find abundant life.
Call us by name
out of our self-inflicted tombs.
Set us free,

that we might live in your presence
with all the saints forever. Amen.

UNISON PRAYER (REVELATION 21)

See, the home of God is among mortals.
God will dwell with them
   and they will be a holy people.
God will be with them
   and will wipe away every tear from their eyes.
Death will be no more.
Mourning and crying and pain will be no more,
   for the first things have passed away.
   Almighty God,
      you have chosen to dwell with us,
      and through your presence,
         you transform the world.
   Teach us how to live in your kingdom,
      that we may put away former ways of death
      and dwell in peace with all people
         in your holy presence. Amen.

BENEDICTION (ALL SAINTS)

The blessing of God,
   the communion of all the saints,
   and the joy of the Savior
   be upon you this day
   and forevermore. Amen.

BENEDICTION (ALL SAINTS)

By the power of Jesus Christ, we are one
with the saints of the past, present, and future.
   May the saints of the past instruct us well,
   that we may be the saints of today,
   and teach the saints of tomorrow.
May this be your task and delight today and forever.

NOVEMBER 5, 2006

Twenty-second Sunday after Pentecost
Christine S. Boardman

COLOR
Green

SCRIPTURE READINGS
Ruth 1:1-18; Psalm 146:1-10; Hebrews 9:11-14; Mark 12:28-34

THEME IDEAS
The story of Ruth's determination to love Naomi is a fitting backdrop to Mark's gospel, where love of God, self, and neighbor takes center stage. In this world of confronting our differences, the stage often is dominated by divisiveness and death, certainly not love. Once again our devotion to Jesus and our understanding of him as mediator is key to our well-being in this world. We come to worship and especially to prayer with renewed appreciation for God's steadfast and unconditional love. As we wander and wonder through our lives, let us cling to our determination to keep love at the center.

CALL TO WORSHIP (HEBREWS 9, MARK 12)
Come, brothers and sisters in Christ,
let us worship the Sovereign God.
We come to proclaim God's goodness
and to follow God's ways.

Come, let us be reminded of all that we have and enjoy.
We come with gratitude: for what is
and for what is to come.
Come, let us hear the message of Jesus for our lives.
We come to learn about Christ as mediator.
The Sovereign has given us freedom to love.
We come to know the love of God, self, and neighbor.
Let us worship together.

CONTEMPORARY GATHERING WORDS (RUTH 1, MARK 12)

Greetings, one and all.
Welcome, neighbors, to God's house.
We are called God's beloved community.
We gather to celebrate our good fortune.
Our questions to Jesus are answered.
Will we hear the commanding message?
The message is to love all of creation.
There are no exceptions.
Sovereign God, the truth is hard.
Teach us to know how to respond to your commandments.

PRAISE SENTENCES (RUTH 1, PSALM 146, MARK 12)

Sing God's praise.
Shout for joy.
Sow the seeds of love.
Share God's goodness.
And let the people say, amen!

OPENING PRAYER (MARK 12, HEBREWS 9)

Sovereign God of the universe,
we enter this place
grateful for your abiding presence.
We are mindful of our need to love,
and our need to be loved.

234

Help us navigate life's challenges wisely,
  basing our decisions on love,
    not on personal gain alone.
Like Jesus,
    may we answer the hard questions of life
    with a strong conviction
      to serve the greater good.
May this worship help us gain strength
    and go the distance
      with love in our sights.
In the name of Christ, our mediator, we pray.
Amen.

PRAYER OF CONFESSION (RUTH 1)

It is time to confess our humanity before our neighbors
  and before our gracious God.
Let us be true to our best selves as God sees us.
Let us be free to speak the truth in love.
  Turn us once again to our interior lives,
    for we know we need not hide from you.
  Too often, our habits hurt rather than help.
  Heal us, O God.
  Help us to receive love from others
    especially when we least expect it.
  Help us to focus on what we have now,
    rather than what we left behind to follow Jesus.
  When we feel like strangers,
    welcome us into your loving embrace.
  When we try to ignore the stranger,
    give us the courage to reach out
      and to be a friend of Christ to them.
  We ask these things in the name of Jesus,
    who went the distance,
      and found you every step of the way. Amen.

WORDS OF ASSURANCE

How good it is to be honest and face our humanity
   in this sacred place.
God loves this world more than any of us can imagine.
Do you know that?
God will not harm you.
Do you know that?
Be at peace for God is pleased when we are honest.
Go in peace wrapped in the garment of forgiveness.

BENEDICTION (MARK 12)

As we prepare to leave this place,
   let us love this world with renewed energy
      and understanding.
Let us trust our Sovereign God
   to lead and guide us.
God is with us; we are not alone.
Go with the blessings of our Creator,
   Redeemer, and Sustainer. Amen.

NOVEMBER 12, 2006

Twenty-third Sunday after Pentecost
Judy Schultz

COLOR
Green

SCRIPTURE READINGS
Ruth 3:1-5; 4:13-17; Psalm 127 (or Psalm 42); Hebrews 9:24-28; Mark 12:38-44

THEME IDEAS
The book of Ruth illustrates God's amazing way of pro- viding for our needs, using the least likely source, Ruth the Moabite, to restore the spirits and hopes of Naomi, the bitter widow. Psalm 42 is a prayer of spiritual distress in which the psalmist acknowledges a deep need for God's refreshing and sustaining care: "As a deer longs for flow- ing streams, so my soul longs for you, O God." What do our congregations need from God today? And how do they understand their need? Mark tells the story of the condemnation of the religious hypocrites and the trusting faithfulness of the widow, who puts all she has to live on into the temple treasury. Are we being called to live sacri- ficially? Or does this widow's gift reflect the tyranny of the temple officials who "devour widows' houses"?

CALL TO WORSHIP (PSALM 42)
Whether you are a member or visitor,
you are welcome here.

**We have come seeking God
and the community of God's people.**
As the deer longs for flowing streams,
so our souls long for God.
**We acknowledge that this deep longing
has brought us to this place.**
Drink deeply of God's love,
for God is here to satisfy our need.
**We will satisfy our soul's thirst,
as we worship the living God.**

CALL TO WORSHIP (PSALM 127)

When our work seems fruitless,
and we are burdened with cares and worry,
**we come into worship,
and take our Sabbath rest.**
When we need rest from our efforts,
and we are tired and discouraged,
**we come into worship,
and take our Sabbath rest.**
Let us worship God together.

CONTEMPORARY GATHERING WORDS (RUTH 3–4)

We warmly welcome you,
to this house of worship.
There are no strangers here,
only friends we have not yet met.
Join in our singing, praying, and listening,
and God will surely bless you
with what you need.
Whatever brought you here,
know that in God's name
you are deeply welcome!
Let us worship God together!

PRAISE SENTENCES (PSALM 127)

Unless God is our strength,
  we are weak.
Unless God is our peace,
  we are at war.
Unless God is our health,
  we are sick.
Unless God is our purpose,
  we wander aimlessly.
Unless God is the very ground of our lives,
  we are not really living.
Unless God is at the center of our worship,
  we worship in vane.
Let us worship God,
  who is our strength, peace, health, and purpose—
    the center of our lives and worship.

OPENING PRAYER (RUTH 3–4, MARK 12)

O God,
  open our hearts
    to your great love this day.
Open our minds
  to hearing your word of truth,
    both of comfort and confrontation.
And open the doors
  of our churches and our homes,
    that we might welcome the stranger,
    embrace the foreigner in our midst,
    and learn to love our enemies.
For in your love,
  we are made one with you,
  with each other,
  and with all the world. Amen.

UNISON PRAYER OR PRAYER OF CONFESSION (RUTH 3–4, MARK 12)

O God of widows and orphans,
     forgive us when we look away from their need.
O God of the homeless and the jobless,
     forgive us when we care only about our own careers,
     and about the accumulation of our own wealth.
O God of the hungry and the despairing,
     forgive us when we ignore the hungry in our own midst
     and when we put our hope in things that do not endure.
Inspire us to work for justice and mercy
     in our cities and neighborhoods.
Forgive us when we refuse to care.

WORDS OF ASSURANCE (MARK 12)

The God who has blessed us with an abundance of love
     forgive our self-centeredness
          when we will turn away from our own needs
          and consider the needs of others.
If we will choose this day
     to live a new life of compassion and care,
          then we are surely forgiven.
May this be a day of new beginnings!
In Jesus Christ, our sins are forgiven!

BENEDICTION

Go from this place with the confidence
     that God has met you here.
Go with the assurance that God has blessed you,
     and will be your spirit's companion on your journey.
Go in joy; go in peace,
     to love and serve the world that God abundantly loves.

BENEDICTION (HEBREWS 9, MARK 12)

Go confidently from this place of worship.
God has blessed you with new life.

We go chastened and empowered.
Go peacefully from this place of worship.
God has blessed us with reconciliation.
We go in peace and gratitude.
Go boldly from this place of worship.
God has work for you to do in the world.
**We go with confidence, to serve God
and God's people in the world.**

NOVEMBER 19, 2006

Twenty-fourth Sunday after Pentecost
Sara Dunning Lambert

COLOR
Green

SCRIPTURE READINGS
1 Samuel 1:4-20; 1 Samuel 2:1-10 (or Psalm 113); Hebrews 10:11-14 (15-18), 19-25; Mark 13:1-8

THEME IDEAS
Hannah's faith leads her out of the depths of despair. With fervent prayers, Hannah begs God to heal her barrenness and send her the son she so desperately wants. The birth of Samuel provides her with the joy and exultation reflected in the Song of Hannah. Similarly, the psalmist praises our strong and benevolent Lord. In Hebrews, we learn that no sacrifice made by priests can cleanse our sins. Only by the perfect sacrifice of Christ are we washed clean of our iniquity. By faith, hope, and love we can follow "the Way." In Mark, Jesus foretells the destruction of the temple and the unrest of the coming days when many followers will be led astray. With prayer as our foundation, we can begin our journey toward a mature faith as followers of Christ—a journey often fraught with stumbling blocks that are difficult to comprehend.

CALL TO WORSHIP (1 SAMUEL 1, 1 SAMUEL 2)

Come worship the Lord who is in our midst today.
There is no Holy One like our God.
Like Hannah of old, we raise our voices
to praise the Lord of strength.
There is no Rock like our God.
We prepare to listen and learn
with open hearts and open minds.
There is no Source of Knowledge like our God.
We trust that righteousness will come
on the heels of God's judgment.
There is no Justice like our God.
May the Son of our God lead us into faith.
There is no Guide like our God.
Come worship the Lord who is in our midst today.

CALL TO WORSHIP (HEBREWS 10, MARK 13)

Let us prepare to hear God's word,
and to accept the sacrifice of Christ for our lives.
We pray for faith with our hearts sprinkled clean,
like the dawn of a new day.
The Holy Spirit has set a covenant before us.
The Lord has written God's laws in our hearts and
minds.
We ask for hope in times of need, in times of want,
and in times of despair.
With the blood of Jesus, the way is opened for us.
Let us not go astray.
We yearn for love, and gather to encourage
each other along God's path. Amen.

CALL TO WORSHIP (HEBREWS 10)

Awake! The time has come to pick up your cross
and follow the way to life!
We approach God with a true heart,
in full assurance of faith.

Through Christ, we enter God's kingdom
washed clean of our sins.
**We pray for the healing waters of Christ
to pour down upon us.**
As we journey together, let us join hands in love.
Amen!

CONTEMPORARY GATHERING WORDS (HEBREWS 10, MARK 13)

Morning has come. A new day is dawning!
We are washed clean with the pure water of Christ.
Despite our troubles, God loves us today!
We are washed clean with the pure water of Christ.
With faith, we come to worship!
We are washed clean with the pure water of Christ.
With hope, we know of God's faithfulness!
We are washed clean with the pure water of Christ.
With love, we teach each other the Way.
We are washed clean with the pure water of Christ.

PRAISE SENTENCES (1 SAMUEL 2)

There is no Rock like our God!
There is no Holy One like the Lord our God!
The God of strength shares our grief.
The God of power listens to our sorrow.
Exalt in the victory of God's might!
God's judgment brings justice to all.
Christ is the way, the life, and the power!

OPENING PRAYER (1 SAMUEL 1, 1 SAMUEL 2)

Through the fervent prayers
of a mother yet to be,
Hannah proved her faith
in the God of strength and justice.

Let us follow her example,
    watching for God's message
        to become clear in our lives today.
Amen!

OPENING PRAYER (HEBREWS 10, MARK 13)
May the Holy Spirit
    join with us today,
     leading us toward faith,
     nurturing our hope,
      and surrounding us with love.
As the scriptures tell us time and again,
    God's abiding love
     sent Christ to us
      to wash away our sins.
Now we must do our part
    to stay on the path together. Amen.

UNISON PRAYER (1 SAMUEL 2, HEBREWS 10)
Gracious Father,
    we join together in songs of praise,
    raising our voices in joyful anticipation
     of your victory in the world.
There is no Rock,
    no holy one besides you.
You are as solid as a mountain,
    as faithful as a mother,
     and bring justice down like a king.
We thank you for the gift of your Son,
    who cleanses us in mind, body, and spirit.
May we walk in your ways,
    and guide each other along the path. Amen.

BENEDICTION (1 SAMUEL 1, 1 SAMUEL 2)
Go in peace, remembering a mother's faith in God—
    a faith that provided her with comfort and strength

in her time of need.
May you pray unfailingly, grow steadily,
and love constantly. Amen.

BENEDICTION (HEBREWS 10, MARK 13)

Depart in the assurance
that Christ has washed away your sins
in the pure water of his blood.
Although the mightiest temple cannot stand forever,
our faith will see us with him in heaven.
In love, we continue the work God started,
so that we will not be led astray.

NOVEMBER 23, 2006

Thanksgiving Day

Rebecca Gaudino

COLOR

Red or White

SCRIPTURE READINGS

Joel 2:21-27; Psalm 126; 1 Timothy 2:1-7; Matthew 6:25-33

THEME IDEAS

Our readings hold together two experiences in life that seem at odds with each other: the experience of human need and sorrow, and the experience of God's lavish love and care. Speaking to a famine-struck people, the prophet Joel contends that the God-ordained rhythms of creation will reestablish themselves in abundance. To "those who sow in tears," the psalmist tells stories of God's goodness, and then promises sheaves of joy. The writer of 1 Timothy holds forth a vision of unity, where all people are reconciled to God. In Matthew, Jesus invites those who are oppressed by worry to imagine life as a bird or a lily—worry free and reliant on God's care alone. These readings do not deny sorrow, need, loss, and anxiety. Instead, they invite us to remember God's provision in the past, and to expect God's love to provide for us today.

CALL TO WORSHIP (JOEL 2, PSALM 126)

Be glad and rejoice in the Lord our God!
God has poured down abundant rain for us.
The trees bear their fruit.
The threshing floors are full of grain.
The vats overflow with wine and oil.
We will eat in plenty and be satisfied.
The earth provides all we need to live.
God has done great things for us!
Be glad and rejoice in the Lord our God!

CONTEMPORARY GATHERING WORDS (MATTHEW 6, JOEL 2)

Look at the birds of the air!
They fly free of our worries,
no fields to weed and harvest,
no barns to fill.
And yet God feeds them.
Consider the lilies of the field!
They grow free of our worries,
no clothing to buy, no shoes to match.
And yet God clothes them in splendor.
So do not worry! Do not fear!
God knows our needs.
We will eat in plenty!
We will be satisfied!
Rejoice, God looks after our needs!

PRAISE SENTENCES (PSALM 126, MATTHEW 6, JOEL 2)

Those who go out weeping,
shall come home with shouts of joy!
Those who worry about their life,
shall learn that God knows all their needs.
Those who have experienced the swarming locust,
shall eat in plenty and be satisfied.

Those who long for comfort,
shall be glad and rejoice,
for God has done great things!

Unison Prayer (Joel 2, Psalm 126, Matthew 6, 1 Timothy 2)

Maker of Heaven and Earth,
    you enliven your creation,
    causing the skies to rain,
    the soil to be rich and fertile,
    the fields to yield abundant crops,
        and the trees to bear fruit.
Enliven us,
    calling us from tears to shouts of joy,
    from calamity to plenty,
    from worry to faith,
    and from what is false
        to what is true.
You who are in our midst;
    you are our God,
        there is no other.
We praise your name,
    for you have dealt wondrously with us
        and will do so again. Amen.

Opening Prayer (Joel 2, Matthew 6, Psalm 126, 1 Timothy 2)

We gather before you today, O God,
    intent on giving you thanks.
We remember the wonders of your past,
    even as we look forward to the wonders
        you have in store for us.
We give you thanks for your mercy and care.
Yet, there are many of us, O God,
    whose lives are sown with tears.
There are rulers and authorities

who do not strive for your kingdom
or your righteousness.
Restore our fortunes, O God,
like streams watering the wilderness,
that we may reap with shouts of joy
what was planted in sorrow. Amen.

PRAYER OF THANKSGIVING (PSALM 126, JOEL 2, 1 TIMOTHY 2, MATTHEW 6)

Persistent in your longing,
unflagging in your blessing,
relentless in your mission,
you know us and our world intimately—
our needs, our hopes, and our failings.
And your great purposes proceed—
the rains return,
the land heals,
destroying armies disappear,
tears give way to laughter,
and humankind is reconciled to you.
We set aside our preoccupation—
our appearance,
the bills,
and the length of our lives.
We set them aside in wonder—
in awe at your grandeur,
the immensity of your dreams,
and the vastness of your intentions.
We give you thanks,
Giver of all blessings, Reason for our hope.
Amen.

BENEDICTION (MATTHEW 6, PSALM 126, JOEL 2)

Know in your depths that you are of great value to God.
**Let us not worry about what we will eat,
what we will wear, and how long we will live.**

For God has done great things for us.
Let us be glad and rejoice in our Sovereign God!
We go in thanksgiving, faith, and joy.

BENEDICTION (PSALM 126, MATTHEW 6)

Go home with shouts of joy!
For God, who has restored us in the past,
will do so again!
Let us go home with shouts of joy!
Go home with shouts of joy!
For God, who knows our tears,
will not leave us comfortless.
Let us go home with shouts of joy!
Go home with shouts of joy!
For God, who knows our needs and daily cares,
will provide us with the blessings of life.
Let us go home with shouts of joy!

NOVEMBER 26, 2006

Christ the King
Reign of Christ Sunday
B. J. Beu

COLOR
White

SCRIPTURE READINGS
2 Samuel 23:1-7; Psalm 132:1-12; Revelation 1:4b-8; John 18:33-37

THEME IDEAS
Human and divine kingship focus today's readings. Though a flawed vessel, King David was everything a human king ought to be. In 2 Samuel, David's last words are an oracle, proclaiming the commitment of his house and lineage to God's everlasting covenant. David trusted the Lord. In Psalm 132, David forswears sleep until a resting place is found for the ark of God. David pledges that God's priests will lead in righteousness, and the people will be taught the ways of the Lord. Yet, David's piety and even God's promise of an everlasting covenant is not enough to keep David's line from falling into sin. Divine kingship alone is sufficient to remain faithful. The readings from Revelation 1 and John 18 herald this kingship. Ultimately, all human kings fail us. Christ alone is our rightful king and sovereign.

CALL TO WORSHIP (2 SAMUEL 23)

The spirit of the Lord speaks to us,
teaching us lessons that endure.
The King of kings calls to us,
beckoning us to follow.
The Light of light shines on us,
illuminating the footsteps of the godly.
The Spirit of the Lord speaks to us,
leading us into life.

CALL TO WORSHIP (JOHN 18)

Christ came to be our king.
We have come to be Christ's people.
Who will worship the sovereign Christ?
We will not turn away.
Come, let us worship the Lord of Life.

CONTEMPORARY GATHERING WORDS (PSALM 132)

God offers us rest.
But where is God's resting place?
We offer the tabernacle of our hearts.
We worship at God's footstool.
But where do we find God's footprints?
We see them in the paths of the righteous.
King David would not sleep
until the ark of God found a resting place.
We will not rest until God abides in our hearts.

PRAISE SENTENCES (REVELATION 1)

God was and is and is to come.
God's love never ends.
God is the Alpha and the Omega.
Christ's love never ends.
God is ruler over all the earth.
The Spirit's love never ends.

PRAISE SENTENCES (JOHN 18)

Our king has come.
Worship Christ the King.
Our king has come.
Worship Christ the King.
Our king has come.

OPENING PRAYER (REVELATION 1, 2 SAMUEL 23)

God who was and is and is to come,
   we approach your throne
     to behold your glory.
Open our eyes,
   that we might witness your Son
   coming with the clouds,
   to rule with justice
     and righteousness.
Open our hearts,
   that we may rejoice
   in your covenant,
   like the sun rising
     on a cloudless morning. Amen.

OPENING PRAYER OR PRAYER OF CONFESSION (JOHN 18, REVELATION 1)

Almighty God,
   we are fascinated with royalty
   and the trappings of power and prestige.
We eagerly follow Britain's royal family
   in newspapers and magazines,
   and secretly enjoy hearing of their scandals.
Forgive us when we lose sight
   that Jesus is our true and only king.
Forgive us when we pay more heed to earthly gossip,
   than heavenly truth.
Help us reaffix our gaze on Christ's kingdom,
   that we might work to bring God's reign here on earth.

In the name of the Alpha and Omega,
the first and the last, we pray. Amen.

ASSURANCE OF PARDON (PSALM 132)
The Lord swore an oath to King David,
  promising faithfulness to his descendants.
In Christ, we have a new covenant,
  assuring us of forgiveness of sins
    and fullness of grace.
In Christ, our true king,
  our lives are made whole.

BENEDICTIN (2 SAMUEL 23, PSALM 132, REVELATION 1)
The Mighty One of Jacob sends us forth.
  We go with God's blessing.
The Rock of Israel sends us forth.
  We go with God's blessing.
The Alpha and Omega sends us forth.
  We go with God's blessing.

BENEDICTION (2 SAMUEL 23, JOHN 18)
God is faithful. God's promises are sure.
  God's kingdom never ends.
Christ is loving. Christ's promises are sure.
  Christ's kingdom never ends.
The Spirit is giving. The Spirit's promises are sure.
  The Spirit's kingdom never ends.
Go with the promises of God.

DECEMBER 3, 2006

First Sunday of Advent
Jack P. Miller

COLOR
Purple or Blue

SCRIPTURE READINGS
Jeremiah 33:14-16; Psalm 25:1-10; 1 Thessalonians 3:9-13; Luke 21:25-36

THEME IDEAS
Darkness is the theme of this day, the first Sunday of the Christian year. It is even called "Somber Sunday" in some circles. Days are short, nights are long, and the sun seems distant—at least in the Northern Hemisphere. The Hebrew prophets eloquently speak of the people walking in darkness, awaiting a great light—the star that will come forth from Jacob. Worship planners will want to strike a dramatic balance between the themes of darkness and light. Some church members impatiently lust to get on with the festivities of Christmas, but it is not Christmas yet. This unique first Sunday of Advent can be a teaching moment about the need for, and nature of, the light that is coming.

CALL TO WORSHIP (ADVENT, ISAIAH 61:1, ISAIAH 40:3, LUKE 4:18, LUKE 3:4)

The Spirit of the Lord is upon us:
to bind up the broken-hearted,
to proclaim liberty to the captives,
to release the prisoners,
to comfort all who mourn,
to repair the ruined cities.
Prepare the way of the Lord.
Build for God a highway in the wilderness.

CONTEMPORARY GATHERING WORDS (ADVENT, LUKE 4:18, ISAIAH 40:3)

Now Advent has begun,
a season in its own right,
not just a countdown to Christmas.
Without Advent,
there would be no Christmas.
So hear the prophet's instructions:
"Prepare the way of the Lord.
In the wilderness make a highway for God."
What wilderness?
Many are drowning in spiritual clutter.
We need help.
We need a Season to cut through it all
like a laser knife,
and point us to the One who is coming.
Come, Lord Jesus!

PRAISE SENTENCES (LUKE 21, ADVENT)

Keep me watching for the coming of the Lord.
Give me oil in my lamp.
Let me stay awake.
Keep me burning 'til the break of day.

OPENING PRAYER (JEREMIAH 33, LUKE 21, ADVENT)

Give to us all, dear God,
a sense of your presence and peace.
In the dark night of the world's anguish,
we pray to you out of our need.
Hear us as we come, intensely alone,
yet holding hands in the darkness,
making one another's cares our own.
Strengthen the poets, the prophets, the peacemakers,
the dreamers, and the dancers of life.
Surprise us today by a new star
that lights up the sky,
giving us hope
and banishing our despair.
In the name of the One who is coming. Amen.

OPENING PRAYER (ADVENT, ISAIAH 40:11)

Your season comes, Lord.
Come once again,
and feed your flock like a shepherd.
Come once again,
and gather up the children, the oppressed,
the sick, the lonely, the humble,
and the rejected of the earth.
Turn our hearts to the least of your children.
For if we lose them,
we become lost.
Reconcile us to you
and to those we have hurt.
At this Advent,
join us together with neighbors, with strangers,
and especially with our own household.
Bring us to your light
in our time of darkness,
through your Son, Jesus Christ. Amen.

PRAYER OF CONFESSION (PSALM 25)

O God,
> you love us into life
> and long for our wholeness.

We confess that our failures are many.
Bless all that we have done which is good,
> and root out all that pulls us down,
> all that moves us toward our dark side.

Lead us into new life,
> that each day will bring some conquest,
> and each night will bring restful sleep,
>> through Jesus Christ our Lord. Amen.

WORDS OF ASSURANCE (EZEKIEL 36:26)

This is the promise: "A new heart I will give you, and a new spirit I will put within you; and I will remove from [you] the heart of stone, and give you a heart of flesh."
In the name of Jesus Christ, you are forgiven!
In the name of Jesus Christ, you are forgiven!

CONTEMPORARY WORDS OF ASSURANCE (PSALM 25, ADVENT)

In the night, we went astray.
> **In the darkness, mercy found us.**
Christ restored us.
Love embraced us.
> **The past is over and gone.**
> **Our future is wide open!**
Let us go and sin no more.

BENEDICTION (2 PETER 1:19, ADVENT)

Pay attention until the day dawns,
> and the morning star rises in your hearts
> like a lamp shining in the darkness.

BENEDICTION (JOHN 1:5, ADVENT)
The light shines in the darkness,
  and the darkness has not overcome it.
Go in grace, to walk in the light.

BENEDICTION (1 THESSALONIANS 3)
Go—be a servant people in the world.
Every day, in every way,
  show and tell the love of Christ,
    the light of the world.

DECEMBER 10, 2006

Second Sunday of Advent

Judy Schultz

COLOR
Purple or Blue

SCRIPTURE READINGS
Malachi 3:1-4; Luke 1:68-79; Philippians 1:3-11; Luke 3:1-6

THEME IDEAS
In Malachi and John, God's message stings, like lye soap or a harshly bristled brush. While the advent of the Messiah is marked with hopeful expectation, preparing for that arrival is not easy or painless. John the Baptist warns us to repent—warning us with words that are forceful, confronting our complacency. We repent because Christ is coming—and in this coming there is hope, eagerness, and anticipation. (B. J. Beu)

CALL TO WORSHIP (MALACHI 3, LUKE 3)
This is a time of great preparation.
What have you come expecting today?
We have come to hear the words
of God's messengers.
Listening to God's messengers is often difficult.
Are you prepared to hear hard truths?
We have come to hear God's truth,
and to receive it as good news.

God's word of confrontation is always followed
by a word of grace.
**Let us hear those words with gladness
as we worship together.**

CALL TO WORSHIP (LUKE 3)

Prepare the way of the Lord.
We are here, prepared to worship.
Prepare the way of the Lord.
We are here, with open hearts.
Prepare the way of the Lord.
We are here, with open minds.
Prepare the way of the Lord.
We are here, open and ready to worship.

CONTEMPORARY GATHERING WORDS (MALACHI 3, LUKE 3)

Gather together, beloved people of God.
**We are prepared to receive God anew
into our lives.**
Gather together, beloved people of God.
**We are open to the light of God
illuminating our lives.**
Gather together, beloved people of God.
**We expect God to appear suddenly,
with great surprises.**
Gather together, beloved people of God!

PRAISE SENTENCES (LUKE 3)

Praise God!
God is coming again with new power.
Prepare for God's coming.
Praise God for never forgetting us.
Praise God for coming to us again and again.

OPENING PRAYER (LUKE 1)

Holy God,
   your tender mercies shine upon us
      like the dawn of a new day.
Your light is the hope of all
   who sit in darkness,
      in the shadow of death.
Be present in our worship this day,
   and guide our feet into the way of peace.
Amen.

OPENING PRAYER (LUKE 1)

O God of Advent and adventure,
   come again into our lives.
We wait for you in darkness
   and in the shadow of death.
We live in troubled times,
   where wars and conflicts
      never seem to cease.
Guide our feet
   in the ways of peace. Amen.

UNISON PRAYER OR PRAYER OF CONFESSION (LUKE 1, 3)

Holy and loving God,
   we have dwelt in darkness
      and preferred it to the light;
   we have been proud of our accomplishments
      and despaired over our shortcomings.
Smooth down the mountains of our pride,
   and lift up the valleys of our doubts.
Open a path in the wilderness of our lives
      that we might find our way to you again.
Refine us and prepare us once again
   for life in your kingdom.
Hear our prayer, O Lord. Amen.

WORDS OF ASSURANCE (PHILIPPIANS 1)
God loves you so much
that in the day of Christ's coming
you will be made pure and blameless.
Accept God's forgiveness,
and reap the harvest of righteousness
that comes from life in Christ.
In the name of God, you are forgiven!

BENEDICTION (PHILIPPIANS 1)
You are God's messenger for this time.
Go out to prepare the way of God in the world.
Make a new beginning,
by forgiving those who have wronged you.
Go in the power of God's forgiving and redeeming love,
bringing forgiveness and redemption
to your homes, neighborhoods, and cities.
Go in the peace of God. Amen.

BENEDICTION (PHILIPPIANS 1)
God has begun a good work in you,
that you alone can accomplish.
**This is good news, but it is a frightening
responsibility to bear.**
God has called and equipped you
to do great things in Christ's name.
**We go with confidence, to proclaim
the good news of Christ's coming.**
Go in joy. Go in peace. Go in great expectation.
Go with God. Amen.

DECEMBER 17, 2006

Third Sunday of Advent
Christine S. Boardman

COLOR
Purple or Blue

SCRIPTURE READINGS
Zephaniah 3:14-20; Isaiah 12:2-6; Philippians 4:4-7; Luke 3:7-18

THEME IDEAS
Advent celebrates the theme of God's salvation. Isaiah and Zephaniah encourage us to sing aloud and shout out our joy: God has given the warrior victory, the lame and outcast no longer live in shame. Philippians broadens this theme, encouraging us to rejoice as we experience the peace that surpasses all understanding in Jesus Christ. Salvation, however, is not all fun and games. John the Baptist calls sinners to repent, in fear and trembling of the wrath to come. Salvation is not cheap grace. It comes with judgment. (B. J. Beu)

CALL TO WORSHIP (ISAIAH 12, LUKE 3)
The Lord our God is in our midst.
Let us rejoice in such goodness.
  Yes, we come seeking inner peace,
  longing to sit silently before our God.
The Lord God is our salvation.

Yes, this is good news indeed.
We need to be at home in love.
Strength, might, and renewal are offered by our God.
Yes, let us seek repentance in the sacred waters
of baptism and find redemption in our God.
Come let us worship as God's people.

CALL TO WORSHIP (ZEPHANIAH 3)

Sing aloud, people of God.
God has taken away the judgments against us.
Sing aloud, people of God.
God has saved us from our enemies.
Sing aloud, people of God.
God has restored our fortunes. (B. J. Beu)

CONTEMPORARY GATHERING WORDS (ZEPHANIAH 3)

Come into this space
  to find silence, refreshment,
    and healing.
Don't be afraid,
  for God welcomes us to this holy place.
Stop what you are doing,
  and behold the goodness
    of our loving and mighty God.
God is strong and mighty,
  fair, just, and trustworthy.
Let us gather with this good news,
  and worship together.

PRAISE SENTENCES (ZEPHANIAH 3, PHILIPPIANS 4)

Time to rejoice!
We are loved.
Be glad, and hear the good news.
We are loved.
Time to rejoice!

OPENING PRAYER (PHILIPPIANS 4)

O God of timeless love,
  we gather in this place
  to feel your gentle touch
    and your powerful peace.
This week has been too full or too empty,
  we are here for what you alone can provide.
Let our voices unite in song and praise.
Let our senses come alive
  to the new birth you offer
    to each one of us.
May the fruits of this time
  be a gift to you and to all
    that gather this day in this place.
Amen.

UNISON PRAYER (ADVENT)

Almighty and Everlasting God,
  we thank you for the promise
    of your coming.
We thank you that you gather us
  as your family of faith
    to worship and to proclaim
      your goodness.
While we have been busy,
  you have been hoping
    that we would pause
      and seek your presence.
Why is it that we try to go it alone?
Bring us to this season of preparation
  with expectant hearts.
Open us to your promises,
  that we may be open to others.
In the name of Jesus, we pray. Amen.

BENEDICTION (PHILIPPIANS 4)

Let God's name be on our lips as we say our farewells.
Let us encircle one another and ask for a blessing
as we depart.
Let us offer to one another the promise
to return again to this place.
Let the peace of God, which surpasses all understanding,
guard our hearts and minds in Christ Jesus. Amen.

BENEDICTION (ISAIAH 12)

God is our salvation. Go forth with trust in the Lord.
God is our salvation. We have nothing to fear.
God is our hope. Go forth with the waters of salvation.
God is our hope. We have been washed clean.
God is our life. Go forth with songs of thanksgiving.
God is our life. We have been blessed with love.

DECEMBER 24, 2006

Fourth Sunday of Advent
Mary J. Scifres

COLOR
Purple or Blue

SCRIPTURE READINGS
Micah 5:2-5a; Luke 1:46b-55; Hebrews 10:5-10; Luke 1:39-45

THEME IDEAS
This is a day of anticipation. Micah anticipates the coming of the one who brings peace—the Messiah from Bethlehem. Mary anticipates being part of God's plan for justice and salvation to a hurting world. Elizabeth anticipates the joy that Mary's child will bring to the people of Israel. And the writer of Hebrews anticipates a new understanding of sacrificial theology. All of these anticipatory hopes point toward Jesus, the center of the upcoming Christmas celebrations.

CALL TO WORSHIP (LUKE 1)
My soul magnifies the Lord.
My spirit rejoices in God my Savior!
God has looked upon us with smiles of love and joy.
God has blessed us from generation to generation.
Let us worship and praise our great God of mercy.

CALL TO WORSHIP (MICAH 5, ADVENT)

The time is coming and now is:
the time of the Lord, who comes to save.
The time is coming and now is:
the time of peace, promised by God.
The time is coming and now is:
the time of hope, embodied in Christ.
The time is coming and now is:
the time of joy, blessed by the Spirit.

CONTEMPORARY GATHERING WORDS (LUKE 1)

Come, singing of grace.
Come, dancing with joy.
As Mary once sang God's praises,
so now we are invited to worship
and praise in honor of Christ.
Let us sing and dance with hope!

PRAISE SENTENCES (LUKE 1)

Magnify the Lord. Sing praises to God!
Magnify the Lord. Sing praises to God!
Blessed be the Lord, the fruit of Mary's womb!
Blessed be the Lord, the fruit of Mary's womb!

OPENING PRAYER (MICAH 5, LUKE 1)

Ancient of Days, blessed Child of God,
be with us this day.
Guide us in your path of peace.
Lead us on the journey of faith
that will bring us to rejoice on Christmas Day.
Help us so to believe where we have not seen,
that we may trust in your promises,
like Mary before us.
In your holy name, we pray. Amen.

OPENING PRAYER (MICAH 5)

O come, o come, Emmanuel.
Come to us this day and all days.
Feed your flock in this time of worship
  with your nourishing grace,
  and your strengthening wisdom.
Help us to dwell secure in your arms of love.
Return to us,
    even as we turn with gratitude and hope
    to our Shepherd and Savior. Amen.

UNISON PRAYER (LUKE 1)

Magnificent God,
  look upon us with your loving favor.
Shine upon us with the light of your wisdom.
Strengthen us in our weakness,
  that we might know the power of your love.
Scatter us in our pride,
  that we might learn the humility of servanthood.
Forgive us when we weaken others
  and forget your place in our lives.
Lift us up when we are disheartened,
  and nourish us with your abundant grace.
Help us, O Promised One of Israel,
  to be your people and to serve your world.
Help us to live as an Advent people,
  hopefully expectant, and patiently diligent,
  that we may bring your realm to this earth. Amen.

BENEDICTION (HEBREWS 10)

We have been sanctified and blessed by the gift of Christ.
We give thanks and praise for this precious gift.
Christ goes with us now, offering support for our lives.
Christ goes with us now, leading the way.

BENEDICTION (LUKE 1)

Blessed are you and blessed is the fruit
of God's spirit within you!
**Blessed are you and blessed is the fruit
of God's spirit within you!**
Go forth as people of the promise—
people who bear witness to the good news.
**We go forth to share the good news
with everyone we meet.**
Amen.
Amen.

DECEMBER 24, 2006

Christmas Eve
Robert Blezard

COLOR
White or Gold

SCRIPTURE READINGS
Isaiah 9:2-7; Psalm 96; Titus 2:11-14; Luke 2:1-20

THEME IDEAS
Isaiah's prophecy comes true tonight, when the light of the world comes to a world dwelling in darkness. Jesus is the One long awaited, the Prince of Peace who brings salvation to us all.

CALL TO WORSHIP (ISAIAH 9)
Long we have walked in darkness.
The light of the world is coming.
We have lived in a land of deep darkness.
The light of the world is coming.
We have borne a heavy yoke of burden.
The light of the world is coming.
We have been beaten by the oppressor's rod.
The Prince of Peace will save us.

CALL TO WORSHIP (TITUS 2)
The grace of God has appeared,
bringing salvation to all.

The Spirit trains us to renounce impiety
and worldly passions,
to live lives that are self-controlled,
upright and godly.
We wait for the hope and manifestation
of our God and Savior, Jesus Christ.
Jesus gave himself to redeem us
and to purify for himself a people.

CALL TO WORSHIP (LUKE 2)

Come! Hear the news of great joy!
A child is born to us this day!
Great joy for all people of the earth.
A child is born to us this day!
A Savior, the Messiah, the Lord!
Glory to God in the highest!

CONTEMPORARY GATHERING WORDS (ISAIAH 9)

Come to the light.
We are weary of darkness.
The light brings us life.
We are weary of darkness.
The light fills our souls.
We will walk in God's freedom and light.

PRAISE SENTENCES (PSALM 96, LUKE 2)

Bless the name of the Lord.
God's light vanquishes our darkness.
Sing a new song to the Lord,
a song of good news and great joy.
Ascribe to the Lord all glory.
God has done marvelous things.
Worship the Lord in holiness.
God's Son has set us free.

OPENING PRAYER (ISAIAH 9)

Illuminate us with your holiness, O God,
we have dwelt too long in deep darkness.
Brighten our gloomy souls with your joy, O God,
we have dwelt too long in ignorance and sin.
Let your glorious dawn
end our long night of oppression.
Bring us salvation in your Son. Amen.

OPENING PRAYER (LUKE 2)

Holy and merciful God,
like the shepherds of old,
we listen for news of great joy,
in the words of the herald angels.
You are coming into the world at last.
Open our hearts and our souls, O God,
that we may welcome your Son
into our lives with joy. Amen.

UNISON PRAYER (LUKE 2)

On this holy night, O God,
we turn our hearts to you.
You are our hope, our light, and our salvation.
On this holy night, O God,
we celebrate the joy of your coming,
and yearn to be born anew.
On this holy night, O God,
we celebrate the mystery of your coming,
awed at how you humbled yourself
to be one with us.
On this holy night, O God,
we welcome the Christ Child:
born in a barn among animals,
wrapped in bands of cloth,
and laid in a feeding trough.

On this holy night, O God,
> we rejoice in your Son, Jesus, our Savior.
Amen.

BENEDICTION (ISAIAH 9)

May God's Son, born this night,
> come into your hearts and lighten your darkness.
May God's Son, born this night,
> guide your footsteps, and lighten your burden.
May God's Son, born this night,
> bring you joy and give you peace,
>> now and ever more.
In the name of God the Father, Son and Holy Spirit,
> go with God's blessing.

BENEDICTION

Let your hearts be at peace. Christ is born.
Let your hearts fill with joy. Christ is born.
Let your hearts be thankful. Christ is born.
Let your hearts be hopeful. Christ is born.
May the love of the newborn Christ,
surround and nourish you now and forever. Amen.

DECEMBER 25, 2006

Christmas Day
Sara Dunning Lambert

COLOR
White

SCRIPTURE READINGS
Isaiah 52:7-10; Psalm 98; Hebrews 1:1-4 (5-12); John 1:1-14

THEME IDEAS
We begin Christmas morning by singing for joy. The messenger brings good news of peace and salvation to Jerusalem: "Your God reigns!" The psalmist chimes in, announcing with a new song, victory to all the ends of the earth. The writer of Hebrews praises the excellent name of Christ, the new message of good news from God and of God. In the gospel passage, we read of "the true light which enlightens everyone" coming into the world.

CALL TO WORSHIP (ISAIAH 52, JOHN 1)
We lift up our voices in praise.
The Light of the World is born today!
We sing joyfully of the good news
of the Savior's birth.
Our God reigns in steadfast love.
Break forth together into singing!
We sing joyfully of the good news
of the Savior's birth.

Hear the good news: Christ is born!
The salvation of God has come.
**We sing joyfully of the good news
of the Savior's birth. Alleluia!**

CALL TO WORSHIP (HEBREWS 1, PSALM 98)
Christ is born today! We celebrate together,
with songs of joy echoing through the hills.
Heaven and earth are filled with God's glory.
Christ is born today! The long night is past,
as we bask in the glory of God's light.
Heaven and earth are filled with God's glory.
The victory of the cross is born in our hearts,
as we anticipate with gratitude the gift today brings.
Heaven and earth are filled with God's glory.
Christ is born! Alleluia!
Alleluia! Christ is born!

CONTEMPORARY GATHERING WORDS
Awake from your slumber.
Christ is born! Alleluia!
The angels sing their praises.
Christ is born! Alleluia!
The seas roar and the mountains quake.
Christ is born! Alleluia!
The hills sing together for joy.
Christ is born! Alleluia!

PRAISE SENTENCES
Blessings this Christmas day!
Christ is born! Alleluia!
Let everyone shout and sing for joy.
The Savior has come! Alleluia!
God's steadfast love endures forever.
Christ is born! Alleluia!
The Word became flesh to live among us.

The Savior has come! Alleluia!
The Light of the world is born today!
Christ is born! Alleluia!

OPENING PRAYER (ISAIAH 52, PSALM 98, JOHN 1)

Light of the World,
    we celebrate your birth
        and the hope it brings to all people.
We have heard the herald's trumpet,
    and seen the glory of our salvation.
Your birth overwhelms us,
    filling our lives with promise and joy.
Your light brings judgment on the earth,
    illuminating our temptation
        to hide in the shadows.
Help us love your light more than darkness,
    that we may be known as children of God.
Amen. (B. J. Beu)

OPENING PRAYER

Word become flesh,
    our hearts sing for joy
        as we behold your glory.
Your presence in our midst
    reminds us anew,
    that your steadfast love
        endures forever.
May our lips never cease
    singing your praises.
And may our hearts never fail
    holding you near. Amen. (B. J. Beu)

BENEDICTION

The Light of the World is born today.
The Christ Child is a visible sign
    of God's unfailing love,
        now and always. Amen.

BENEDICTION (PSALM 98)

Go tell it on the mountaintop!
Jesus Christ is born!
The seas roar, the floods clap their hands.
The hills sing together for joy!
Make a joyful noise to the Lord!
Jesus Christ is born!

BENEDICTION (JOHN 1)

The true light that enlightens all has come to us today.
This light was with God in the beginning
    and goes forth with us now.
With the grace of God, go with the joy of knowing
    that Christ the Lord is born!

DECEMBER 31, 2006

New Year's Day

Joanne Carlson Brown

COLOR
White

SCRIPTURE READINGS
Ecclesiastes 3:1-13; Psalm 8; Revelation 21:1-6a; Matthew 25:31-46

FIRST SUNDAY AFTER CHRISTMAS READINGS
1 Samuel 2:18-20, 26; Psalm 148; Colossians 3:12-17; Luke 2:41-52

THEME IDEAS
This is a time of new beginnings—a time to reflect on the promises of newness and possibilities—God is making all things new. It is also a time to reflect that there is a time for everything under heaven. We are called to renew our covenant with God—the covenant to be the people God calls us to be—to be God's hands and feet in the world; and to bring the message that in God's realm, there is comfort, love, justice, and a chance to begin anew.

CALL TO WORSHIP (ECCLESIASTES 3)
For everything there is a season.
We come to worship God with our whole lives.
We celebrate all the times of our lives:

times to laugh and cry, times to dance and mourn,
times of silence and times of speech,
times of war and times of peace.
Come let us worship the God of our times and seasons.

CALL TO WORSHIP (PSALM 8)

Come, people of God. Come and worship our God.
How majestic is your name in all the earth.
Come, people of God. Come and worship the God
who cares for us.
We give thanks to our loving and caring God.
Come, people of God. Come and worship the God
who has crowned us with glory and honor.
We celebrate the God of glory and wonder.

CALL TO WORSHIP (REVELATION 21)

This is the day of new beginnings.
We give thanks for newness of life.
Today, God dwells with us.
We celebrate that we are God's beloved people.
Today, all things are made new.
Let us worship God, the alpha and omega.

CONTEMPORARY GATHERING WORDS (NEW YEAR)

Happy New Year!
We celebrate with our whole lives
the gift of new beginnings.
Come, live into this season of new birth.
God will be with us in all the changes
life will bring this year.
So come, beloved of God,
let us worship the God of our lives.

PRAISE SENTENCES (PSALM 8)

Majestic is God's name in all the earth!
Praise to God, the sovereign of all.

God fills us with glory and honor.
Praise our caring and creating God.

OPENING PRAYER (NEW YEAR)

Ever loving God,
   we come to this new year
   with hopes and dreams,
   fears and doubts.
As we step across the threshold of this new year,
   may we have confidence in your abiding presence
      in all the myriad aspects of our lives.
In this time of worship,
   open us to all the possibilities and promises
      that a new year can bring.
Bring your new heaven and new earth,
   that we may live with you in justice and peace.
We pray this in the name of the God,
   the alpha and omega,
   the one of new beginnings. Amen.

OPENING PRAYER (ECCLESIASTES 3)

O God of all seasons and purposes under heaven,
   we come in this season of new beginnings
   to pray for guidance
      in all the aspects of our lives.
Help us to remember that no matter what happens,
   you are always with us—
   in times of joy and sadness, life and death,
   silence and speech, dancing and mourning,
      war and peace.
May we always live in such a way
   that we reflect the glory to your name.
As we are mindful of the past,
   let us rejoice in the future.
We pray in the name of the God
   of all of our days and ways. Amen.

PRAYER OF CONFESSION (MATTHEW 25)

Ever present, ever loving God,
  we come to this new year
  mindful of the things we have done
  and left undone in the past.
Forgive the times when we did not reach out in love
  to the least of your sons and daughters.
Forgive us O God,
  when we closed our eyes
    to the sight of people
      living in rags on the street;
  when we stopped our ears
  to cries of those who are lonely;
  when we turned away from the sight
  of swollen, malnourished bodies.
Help us to see you in all we meet.
Help us to be your hands, feet, and voice in this world.
May we work for a world where no one will be a stranger,
and all will be welcomed into your eternal glory. Amen.

WORD OF ASSURANCE (MATTHEW 25)

Our God is a God of compassion and love,
  ready to forgive all who truly repent
  and desire to live a life of justice and love.
Know that the God who calls us
  to be members of God's family,
  will welcome you with open arms of grace
    and forgiveness.

BENEDICTION (ECCLESIASTES 3)

Go forth, rejoicing that our God is with us
  in all times and places,
  and in all the seasons of our lives.

BENEDICTION (REVELATION 21)

Go forth into the new year, trusting in God's promises.
And may God, the alpha and the omega,
  be with you always.

CONTRIBUTORS

ERIK ALSGAARD is an ordained elder in the Detroit Conference currently serving as communications director for the Baltimore Annual Conference of the United Methodist Church.

LAURA JAQUITH BARTLETT is a clergy member of the Oregon-Idaho Conference of the United Methodist Church.

B. J. BEU is pastor of Fox Island United Church of Christ in the Puget Sound of Washington. A graduate of Boston University and Pacific Lutheran University, Beu also teaches church history and doctrine for his denomination.

ROBERT BLEZARD is a freelance writer, editor, and Webmaster who does most of his work for the Evangelical Lutheran Church in America. He is working toward ordination as a Lutheran pastor.

CHRISTINE S. BOARDMAN was ordained in 1984 in the United Church of Christ. Prior to ministry, Christine was a professional singer. She has served as pastor to three small rural churches and has specialized in serving as an intentional interim minister for 13 years serving five conferences.

MARY PETRINA BOYD is pastor of Coupeville United Methodist Church on Whidbey Island in Puget Sound. She spends alternate summers working as an archaeologist in Jordan.

JOHN A. BREWER pastors Salmon Creek United Methodist Church in Vancouver, Washington, after serving eight years in the district superintendency.

JOANNE CARLSON BROWN is a United Methodist minister. She is pastor of United Church in University Place (a UCC-UMC joint congregation) and adjunct professor at Seattle University School of Theology and Ministry.

DAVID BUECHLER is a student at Fuller Theological Seminary and a candidate for ordination in the United Methodist Church.

MARK DOWDY is pastor of the United Churches of Olympia, a Federation of the United Church of Christ and the Presbyterian Church (USA), in Olympia, Washington.

REBECCA GAUDINO is a United Church of Christ pastor in Portland, Oregon.

JAMIE GREENING is the Senior Pastor of First Baptist Church, Port Orchard, Washington.

BILL HOPPE is the music coordinator and keyboardist for Bear Creek United Methodist Church in Woodinville, Washington.

SARA DUNNING LAMBERT is the worship coordinator at Bear Creek United Methodist Church in Woodinville, Washington.

JACK P. MILLER is a retired United Methodist pastor, ordained an elder in the South Indiana Conference.

MARY J. SCIFRES pastors Port Orchard United Methodist Church, near Gig Harbor, Washington. She is the author of *Searching for Seekers: Ministry with a New Generation of the Unchurched* and coauthor of *Prepare! A Weekly Worship Planbook for Pastors and Musicians* and *The United Methodist Music and Worship Planner* for Abingdon Press.

BRYAN SCHNEIDER-THOMAS is pastor of Amble United Methodist Church in Lakeview, Michigan and also serves as a liturgical design consultant.

JUDY SCHULTZ has been in ministry in the United Methodist Church for twelve years; she currently is pastor of the Haller Lake United Methodist Church in Seattle, Washington.

CRYSTAL R. SYGEEL is currently serving as pastor of First United Methodist Church in Bellevue, Washington.

SCRIPTURE INDEX

OLD TESTAMENT